THE NATION'S FAMILIES:

1960–1990

A Joint Center Outlook Report

THE NATION'S FAMILIES: 1960–1990

GEORGE MASNICK AND MARY JO BANE

with
Neal Baer
John Pitkin
Lee Rainwater
Martin Rein
Barbara Wiget

Auburn House Publishing Company
Boston, Massachusetts

Library of Congress Cataloging in Publication Data

Masnick, George S   1942–
  The Nation's families, 1960–1990.

  Bibliography: p.
  1.   Family—United States—Statistics.
2.   Households—United States—Statistics.
I.   Bane, Mary Jo, joint author.   II.   Title.
HQ536.M326 1980   306.8'0973   80-20531
ISBN 0-86569-050-2

Printed in the United States of America.

PREFACE

America's cities have been a focus of public concern ever since the massive urbanization of the country began in the nineteenth century. In the past several decades, the shape of urban areas changed: The central cities began to decline as people and jobs moved out; new housing was built in the suburbs, almost all of it single-family; and the composition and location of industrial activity changed markedly. The process has been complicated even further by uneven regional development, with industry and workers migrating to the South and West from the older manufacturing areas. Now, as the country moves toward 1990, energy shortages, persistent inflation, environmental constraints, and a changing population are reshaping the process of urban development in new ways that will have profound implications for our economy and our society.

The Joint Center for Urban Studies was established in 1959 to focus and coordinate research at MIT and Harvard relevant to understanding the process of urban change and the public strategies that might influence it. Since 1971 the Joint Center's research has focused on housing as a central element in the urban development process. The Center sought to understand the underlying dynamics of housing supply as well as the economic and demographic characteristics that influence housing demand. As one product of that research, the Joint Center has produced reports providing a broad outlook on the current status and future of housing demand and supply, the current one of which is *The Nation's Housing: 1975–1985*.

The Joint Center is now expanding its Outlook Report series to encompass all three of its major research areas: housing and community development; regional and urban development; and family and population studies. Since population and household trends are a significant force affecting urban development, housing needs and the other areas of traditional concern for the Joint Center, population and family research is an important component of the Center's program.

The present volume is the first in a series of Outlook Reports on the nation's population, households and families. Research in regional economics is also being undertaken at the Center to improve our understanding of the regional differences in urban change and the relationships among central city, suburban and rural economies. An Outlook Report on regional economies will be issued next year, reporting on the research to date. That report will extend some of the material in the Family Outlook Report to examine regional differences in population and household trends, a topic which we plan to investigate in greater depth over the next few years.

This Family Outlook Report brings together some of the findings of Joint Center research to identify the emerging trends and to interpret their implications. The population trends that produced the "baby boom" of the late 1950s and early 1960s were clearly a driving force in many of the economic and geographic changes of that time. Large proportions of young Americans married early, started what became relatively large families, and moved to the suburbs. They provided a huge market for single-family homes and for the goods and services that the suburban life style required. The better off among them abandoned the cities to the poor, and made the suburbs the major economic and political force in the country.

In 1980 the children of the baby boom are entering young adulthood. Their large numbers hold the potential for an enormous new surge of marriage and childbearing—if they follow the family formation patterns of their parents. But, as this report shows, there are indications that the baby boom young adults are establishing quite different life styles from their parents, with later marriage, fewer children, more divorce, more working wives, and so on. These young adults may, instead of triggering a new suburban expansion and a large demand for additional single family houses, look more toward the cities, toward apartments and condominiums, and toward the goods and services that life in the smaller, more transient household units demand. To the extent this occurs, it will pose new problems and new opportunities for our urban areas.

The authorship of this report was shared as follows: George Masnick was primarily responsible for the research and writing of Chapter 2, and Mary Jo Bane of Chapter 3. Bane and Masnick drafted Chapters 1 and 4 together. Neal Baer provided research assistance for Chapters 3 and 4. John Pitkin contributed substantially to the research reported in Chapter 2 and was primarily responsible for the household projections. Lee Rainwater and Martin Rein contributed substantially to the research in Chapter 3 as well as to the conceptualization of the entire report. Barbara Wigit provided research assistance for Chapters 2 and 3. The authors and collaborators are all participants in the Joint Center's ongoing program of research on population and families. A list of related publications from that program appears in Appendix A.

The authors would like to thank a number of people for their contributions to this report. For overall coordination of the production of the report, Charlotte Moore. For graphics and design, Glenna Lang. For editing, Nancy Lyons. For help with the production process: Anne Aubrey, Irene Goodsell, Richard Harrington, Jan Lent, Carol Scanlon, and Nora Turchi. For comments and discussion at various points in the formulation of the materials and ideas presented here: William Alonso, Tamara Hareven, Laura Lein, Nathan Keyfitz, Lance Liebman, Scott McDonald, John Meyer, Dowell Myers, George Penick, Ronnie Ratner, and Arthur Solomon.

DAVID T. KRESGE
DIRECTOR

CONTENTS

CHAPTER 3
Women's Work and Family Income   52

CHAPTER 4
Changing Families, Changing Times   95

LIST OF FIGURES

LIST OF TABLES

Chapter 1

INTRODUCTION

Awareness of major changes in American family life has been drilled home over the past few years by newspaper and newsmagazine features, television specials, award-winning movies, and—for many—firsthand experience. The drop in marriage rates and the jump in divorce rates are only the tip of the iceberg. Fertility levels have declined, illegitimacy ratios have climbed, women have joined the paid labor force in increasing numbers, and men and women have sought solitary living arrangements to an unprecedented extent. Many conclude that something has gone seriously awry.

What is the appropriate public response to these changing family patterns? To juggle our institutions—education, health care, taxation, housing, work, social security, the law and so on—to accommodate the changing needs of families is seen by some as supporting the very forces that have thrown the family into a tailspin. But to defend current institutional arrangements in these areas or to implement new policies in the hopes of reversing trends in family and household structure that are viewed as undesirable would be to risk swimming against the tide of social change and thereby to ignore the emerging future needs of the American people.

The impediments to designing an informed and sensitive family policy are threefold. First, Americans always have held nostalgically onto the ideals of the traditional family—how family life *ought* to be. Second is the sheer inertia built into established institutions. Vested interests are never quick to support changes in any social institutions. In addition to that general mood, those most directly charged with developing, implementing and paying for new public policies are likely to be middle-aged Americans. They are members of that "lucky" generation who came closer than any other to the ideal of American domesticity: a nice suburban home; a breadwinner

1

husband and a homemaker wife; dedication to childrearing; and status gained from a high level of consumption of housing, automobiles, appliances, and other consumer goods. This generation of adults, now between the ages of 40 and 60, is especially reluctant to validate life styles and family forms so different from its own.

The third source of resistance to changes in our households and families is a genuine lack of understanding of what is happening, and why. Here is the area in which the material presented in this book can make a contribution. The methods we have chosen to analyze selected variables provide new insights into certain trends in population, household, and family structure. We are able to set aside several misconceptions about recently observed changes in the American family and to more confidently predict changes that are in store over the next decade. A deeper level of understanding will enable us all to break down the resistance—both institutional and generational—to making our society more responsive to changing family needs.

Five aspects of the changing American family can be singled out from among our major findings as being particularly significant:

1. Far from being abnormal, the low marriage, high divorce, and low fertility rates of today's generation of young adults are consistent with long-term trends, though inconsistent with the pattern established by their parents' generation.
2. Between now and 1990, households made up of married couples will increase only slightly in number, while other types of households will increase dramatically.
3. Fewer and fewer households will have children present.
4. Although more wives are working, their contribution to family income is small and has not changed.
5. A revolution in the impact of women's work is on the horizon.

Until the 1940s, fertility rates had been consistently falling and marriage rates had begun to level off, while divorce, employment, and household formation rates had been consistently rising. Had the 1940s and 1950s not happened, today's young adults would appear to be behaving normally. Their family formation would reflect a continuation of historical trends. However, when the benchmark chosen to judge the family patterns of today's young adults is that of their parents' generation, those born since 1940 do appear deviant. When men and women born between 1920 and 1940 (age 40–60 in 1980) were young adults, marriages took place much earlier, fertility rates were higher, and divorce rates were lower. But it was the parents' generation that deviated from the historical trends.

In Chapter 2 we examine the ways in which today's generation of middle-aged adults, born between 1920 and 1940, differed in their family building behavior from the generations born before 1920 and after 1940. Of particular interest is the 15-year span of the life course between ages 20 and 35. This period is when major transitions into adulthood take place: establishing a household, entering the labor force, getting married, and having children.

The method we use to compare life-course patterns of generations is called *cohort analysis*. The behavior of a group of individuals born in the same years, a "birth cohort," is followed as it ages. Such data as the proportion of the cohort never-married at each age, or the proportion that became parents, or the proportion currently in the labor force are calculated. Consistent trends from age to age over the cohort's life course, as well as among successive cohorts, allow us to project future trends.

Our analysis indicates that between now and 1990, the generation of young adults will continue to postpone marriage, head their own households, and eventually have smaller families. The middle-aged generation of 40- to 60-year-olds will enter the empty-nest period and significant numbers will become widowed. Among members of the older generation—those over the age of 60 in 1980—widowhood will be even more significant. Rising levels of divorce should occur in all three generations.

The implications of these changes in life course variables for household and family structure are summarized in Figure 1.1, which shows the number of households of different types in 1960 and 1975, and projected to 1990: married couples with and without children; male- and female-headed families with and without children; and men and women not heading families.

The changes between 1960 and 1975 were concentrated in three types of households: (1) married couples with no children; (2) female-headed families; and (3) men and women living alone. All categories increased substantially.

Change: 1960–1975

1. 19.7 million more *total households*.
2. 8.0 million more *married couples*.
   —7.1 million *without children* at home.
   —0.9 million *with children* at home.

3. 11.7 million more unattached individuals.
   —3.7 million more *single or previously married men* living alone or with children.
   —2.3 million more *single or previously married women* with children at home.
   —5.7 million more *single or previously married women* not heading families.

Our projections from 1975 to 1990 show an equally large increase in the number of households, but married couples will make up a substantially smaller proportion of that increase.

Change: 1975–1990

1. 20.2 million more *total households*.
2. 3.4 million more *married couples*.
   —0.4 million *without children* at home.
   —3.0 million *with children* at home.
3. 16.8 million more *unattached individuals*.
   —7.0 million more *single or previously married men* living alone or with children.
   —2.6 million more *single or previously married women* with children at home.
   —7.2 million more *single or previously married women* not heading families.

These changes show the population to be more evenly spread across several household types in 1990. Because no one arrangement will be "typical," there will be demands for a wide range of different kinds of housing, consumer goods, and public and private services. As they move through life from youth to old age, people will have more diverse experiences. Men and women will spend fewer years in conventional nuclear families and more years living apart from close relatives. They will move from one type of household to another more frequently than in the past, and will undoubtedly develop greater flexibility in adapting to new ways of life.

Most people will have a variety of family experiences, a point that is important to keep in mind interpreting changes that have occurred and will occur. For example, the fact that 12 percent of the population lives alone at a given point in time (the 1979 figure) does not mean that particular individuals are alone forever. It can mean instead that most of the population lives alone for a short period sometime, often in youth or old age. Similarly, the fact that only 47 percent of people are married at one point in time does not imply that a majority do not marry. Most do, in fact, but at older ages, and with other types of living arrangements before, after, and often in between. People will have more complicated histories and probably more complicated sets of relationships from one stage of life to another.

The generation of young adults born during the baby boom hold the potential for a tremendous surge in marriage and childbearing because of their sheer numbers. From their already established cohort fertility trends, however, we expect this generation to continue the pattern of low fertility throughout the next decade. Perhaps as many as half the women born during the mid-1950s will have passed through their prime childbearing years by 1990 childless or with only one child. When the households headed by these young women and couples without children are added to those from the middle and older generations who were childless or whose children have grown up, a declining proportion of all households will have young children present. By 1990 we expect only half of all husband/wife couples to have children under the age of 15 living at home. The 25 million husband/wife households without children in 1990, when added to the 20 million expected female-headed households without children and the 14 million households headed by men without children present, yield a total of almost 60 million households without children. This figure represents almost two-thirds of the projected total number of 1990 households!

Strongly related to trends in delayed marriage, smaller family size, and independence of living arrangements is the sharp increase in the number of women seeking paid employment outside the home. Employment has enabled women to maintain independent households in their young adult years and to delay marriage if they choose. The rewards of paid work have begun to reach a significant fraction of wives who in the past would have been homemakers most of their adult lives. For the younger wives who are working during their childbearing years, labor force activity is competing with motherhood and tending to lower fertility rates.

The scope of the changes in women's employment behavior can be seen by taking another cut at the distribution of households, this time by whether household heads and spouses in husband/wife families work (Figure 1.2).

Change: 1960–1975

1. Two-worker husband/wife families increase from 23 percent to 30 percent of all households.

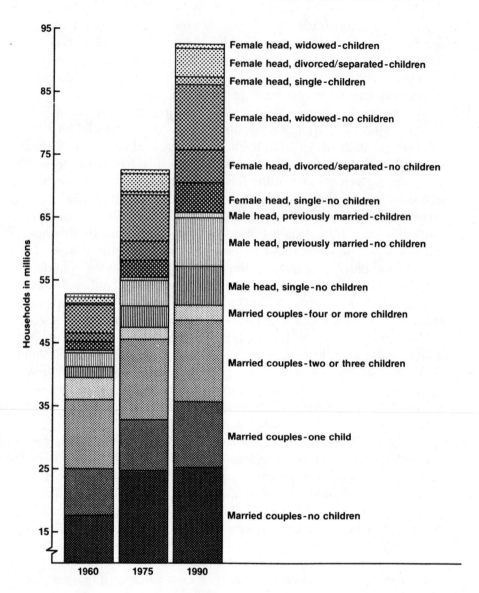

Figure 1.1. Types of Households, 1960, 1975, and 1990. *(Source: Table 2.13.)*

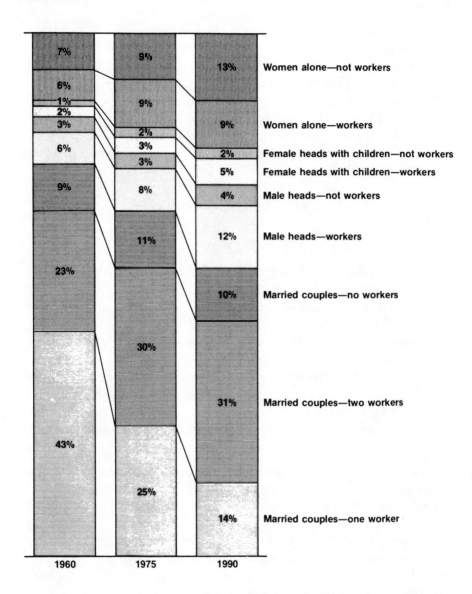

Figure 1.2. Employment Characteristics of Households, 1960, 1975, and 1990. *(Source: Table B. 1.)*

2. No-worker households increase from 20 percent to 25 percent of all households.
3. One-worker households decrease from 57 percent to 45 percent of all households because of two opposing trends:
   —a large drop in one-worker husband/wife households, from 43 percent to 25 percent of households.
   —a jump in one-worker households of other types—female heads and men and women living alone—from 14 to 20 percent of households.

Our projections to 1990, which are conservative, show these trends continuing:

Change: 1975–1990

1. Two-worker husband/wife households increase slightly from about 30 percent to 31 percent of households.
2. No-worker households go from 25 percent to about 28 percent of all households.
3. One-worker households decrease from 45 percent to 40 percent of all households because of:
   —a substantial decrease in one-worker husband/wife households, from 25 percent to about 14 percent of all households.
   —an increase in other types of one-worker households from about 20 percent to 26 percent of all households.

These changes come about mainly because of the increases in the proportion of women who work, not only never-married and previously married women, but also wives and mothers. The change in no-worker households results from an increase in the proportion of households headed by people over 65 and from an increase in the tendency to live alone among other groups who have lower work rates than the general population—that is, young people (some of whom are students) and single parents.

As we shall see, the data on working conceal what may be an even more far-reaching change that is just beginning within families. In 1980 most working women had part-time, part-year jobs or worked intermittently over a period of years. Working wives contributed only about a quarter of family income. Average incomes of female-headed families and of women living alone were much lower than those of men, even in those households where the women worked full time.

The revolution yet to come is in women's attachment: more women working full time more continuously. Greater attachment will, in turn, raise their contributions to family income. Recent trends toward year-round, full-time and continuous work, especially among younger women, make this revolution seem likely. If it does occur—if women develop more substantial and permanent attachment to work—their working in 1990 may trigger important changes in the consumption, time-use, and mobility patterns of families than are now evident.

We project by 1990 a very diverse world of households, families, and individual life histories. Households will be smaller, and they will change more often. There will be more two-worker households and more households of men and women living alone than husband/wife households with one worker. These new kinds of households are likely to change the face of the cities, create markets for quite different kinds of houses and consumer goods, and place new demands on public programs. They will create unprecedented challenges for the economy, for the community, and for the government—challenges that the society must prepare to meet.

Chapter 2

POPULATION, HOUSEHOLDS, AND FAMILIES

In a fashion similar to the alignment of the Sun, Earth, and Moon during a total solar eclipse, three very different generations of adult Americans are now exerting their forces simultaneously to pull and tug at the very foundations of traditional family and household structure. The older generation, born 1920 or before and age 60 or over in 1980, survived the Great Depression. Most have been through two world wars, many were immigrants or sons and daughters of immigrants, and all were born at a time when over half of the U.S. population was rural. They married late, had small families, and today many live alone.

The middle generation, born between 1920 and 1940, and age 40 to 59 in 1980, entered adulthood during a period of optimism and affluence. As if to avenge the injuries history bestowed on the preceding generation, its members married early, bought large cars and houses, gave witness to civil rights, and had babies. Many in this generation are now in the empty-nest stage of their lives, and many are divorced.

The younger generation is made up of the babies born during the "boom" years that began with World War II. Although many in this group of today's under-40-year-olds have only just begun their adult lives, they have already had a profound influence on American family life by virtue of their numbers and life styles. They have begun to settle down in the central cities and in small towns, two areas abandoned by their parents. More of the women have put independence and work before marriage and childbearing, and men and women are better educated than earlier generations. In these and other ways, this younger group of adults stands in sharp contrast to its parents and grandparents.

The different experiences and unique contributions that each of these generations has offered and will continue to offer as it lives out its life course are directly responsible for changes in the American family and in household patterns: the shrinking size of households; the decline in the proportion of households headed by a married couple; the increase in the number of working mothers; the sharp rise in the number of people who live alone; the jump in divorce rates and in fraction of children living with only one parent; the growing inability of one-earner families to cope with recession and inflation; and the sex and age segregation that characterize our population's living arrangements.

Our analysis distinguishes between *household* and *family*. A family is defined as two or more individuals who live together and are related to one another by blood or marriage. This definition includes husband/wife households (with or without children present) and single-parent households (usually the mother and always with children present). A sprinkling of other family types, such as single adult children who live with one parent and siblings who share the same household, round out the family picture. A household is more broadly defined and consists of one or more people who may or may not be related but who maintain a separate living unit (defined as having its own entrance or cooking facilities). Households therefore include husband/wife and other types of families, but also include people who live alone or with roommates.

Whenever possible, we examine the trends in demographic, household, and family variables that allow us to draw distinctions between the life courses of the three generations. This is called a "cohort" perspective, and traces the actual behavior at each age in the life course of individuals who were born in the same years.

Overview of Trends

The trend away from traditional households and toward more varied living arrangements mirrors the basic age and sex structure of the society. It also reflects specific changes in the makeup of households and families:

1. A shift in the age when children leave home.

2. A rise in the proportion of families made up of women living with children or other relatives but not with husbands.
3. A decline in average household size, and a rise in the proportion of single-person households.
4. A decline in husband/wife households as a proportion of all households.
5. A decline in the number of people who live neither alone nor as nuclear family members—for example, lodgers, boarders, siblings, parents, or grandparents of the couple or individual heading the household.

Figures 2.1 and 2.2 present population pyramids for U.S. households for four years: 1940, 1950, 1960, and 1970. Each pyramid shows the percentage of the population that falls in age groups clustered in 5-year spans from age 0 to 70+. Each age group is further broken down by sex and by the proportion falling into four broad categories of household positions: (1) head of household; (2) wife of head; (3) child of head; and (4) all other individuals outside the nuclear family.[1]

The 1940 pyramid is fairly even on its sides and tapers at the younger age groupings at the bottom, the consequence of a long, gradual decline in both fertility and mortality that began as far back as the first half of the nineteenth century. In the 1950 and 1960 pyramids the bases broaden out, indicating the increase in the percentage of young children in the population added during the post-World War II baby boom.

By 1970 the narrowed base of the pyramid reflects the post-baby boom decline in fertility. The children of the baby boom years, meanwhile, have moved up the pyramid, creating a bulge at the teenage years. By 1980, they fall into the young adult age groups and will swell the ranks of the mature adult years by 1990. The baby boom generation will begin to have an impact on the relative size of the elderly population around the year 2010, when the oldest of them (born in 1945) reaches age 65.

Age Shifts of Children in Population and in Households

We can see by the pyramids that a greater proportion of the children living at home in 1940 were older than those at home in 1950 and 1960. In fact, children over the age of 15 made up almost 17 percent of the household population in 1940, compared with only about 10 percent in 1960. Two developments in the behavior of the middle generation (born between 1920 and 1940) that differed from the life course of the older generation (born 1920 and before) account for this pattern. The first was simply that it left home at an earlier age. The second was its increased fertility, which accounts for the relatively greater number of young children in the population (and at home) by 1950 and 1960. In the population pyramids for those years, the most numerous age group of children were those under 5.

The older generation was part of a long-term trend of declining fertility. That sort of trend eventually leads to a population pyramid where the younger age groupings get smaller each year as the number of births decline. Parallel to this trend, in 1940 there were more 10- to 14-year-olds than youngsters 5–9. The 15- to 19-year-olds were the largest age group of all. After the age of 15, of course, children begin to move out of their parents' households. They marry, enter the armed services, go away to school, or simply live on their own.[2] Thus, even though the 15- to 19-year-olds were the largest age group in 1940, a smaller fraction lived at home than in younger age groups. But compared with 1950, 1960, and 1970, more older children in their late 20s and early 30s still lived with their parents in the years before World War II.

By 1970 the younger generation's declining annual number of births (which had started in 1962) reduced the size of the youngest grouping in the population pyramid, making the 10- to 14-year-olds once again the most numerous. Traditionally, the delayed marriage and childbearing of the younger generation would coincide with a delay in its leaving home. Counteracting that trend, however, has been the move toward increasing independent living among the never-married, especially among those in the younger generation over the age of 25 in 1980. The eventual net trend in how long members of the younger generation, including those under 25, will live at home is still uncertain. The cost of college, employment prospects, and the cost and availability of housing all influence the decision to move, to stay at home, or perhaps to live with parents from time to time.

In contrasting the three generations' experience as young adults, those born before 1920 maintained closer ties with their parents' households. Even young marrieds lived at home with parents, indicating the relatively greater role that parents in the past played in the lives of their adult children. Parental influence undoubtedly extended into the spheres of work (arranging the first job), marriage (greater control over selection of spouse), childrearing and leisure

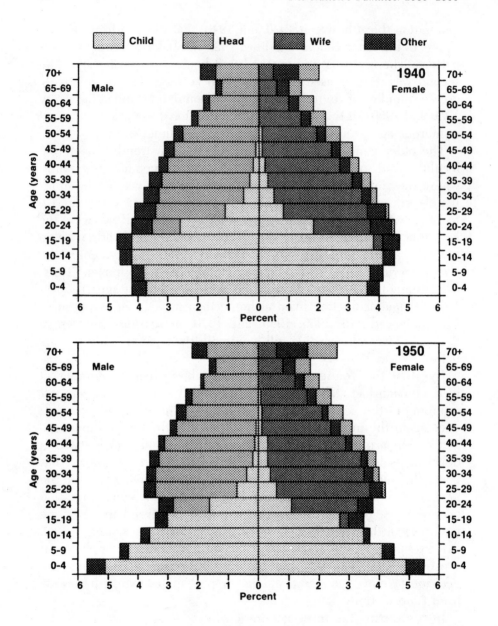

Figure 2.1.   U.S. Population by Household Relationship, 1940 and 1950.
(Source: Appendix Table B.2.)

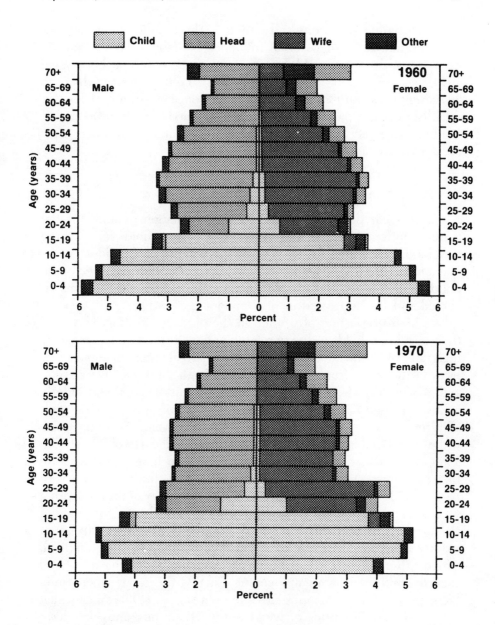

Figure 2.2. U.S. Population by Household Relationship, 1960 and 1970. (*Source: Appendix Table B.2.*)

(extended family vacations and outings). The middle generation cut down certain lines of parental influence by moving away, quickly marrying and having children. The younger generation, born since 1940, has continued to move away from home, but has done so increasingly as *individuals*.[3] Its independence is premised less on establishing the separate responsibilities of marriage, parenthood, and a suburban home than on new life-style ideas about marriage, children, living arrangements, and work.

Rise in the Proportion of Female-Headed Households

A second clear pattern revealed by the population pyramids is the increase in female household heads. This pattern holds for all three generations. It shows up in 1940 among widows of the older generation; in 1950 and 1960 among widows, divorced, and separated of the middle generation; and in 1970, among the never-married, the divorced and the separated of the younger generation.

The high proportion of women in the older generation who head their own households is due to a combination of trends. First are their high rates of widowhood because of the relatively high male mortality rates in the years from World War I through the Great Depression and World War II. In 1940 many of these middle-aged and elderly widows headed families made up of siblings of one or more adult children who helped to maintain the household. Second, many widows of the older generation who were over the age of 55 in 1950, 1960, and 1970 were forced to head their own households because they had fewer surviving children who could take them in. They were part of the low-fertility generation, and the number of their offspring was reduced further by the high mortality rates during the years of the Depression and the two world wars. A third reason why more elderly women head their own households today is their ability to support themselves through survivors' benefits from pensions, social security, and their own employment. Finally, the greater increase in life expectancy for women relative to men since 1940 has meant that an ever-greater number of wives outlive their husbands and have longer periods of widowhood. By their late 70s and early 80s, many women in the older generation in the 1970 pyramid had not only outlived their husbands but also had survived their children.[4]

Female heads of households are often (but not always) heads of families, which means they live with children, siblings, or parents who are dependent upon them in a variety of ways. Table 2.1 gives

Table 2.1. Families Headed by Women without Husbands Present

	Marital Status (Percentages)				Percentage of All Families Headed by Women
Year	Husband Absent	Single	Divorced	Widowed	
1940	12.9	16.9	7.4	62.8	15.1
1950	16.1	11.6	12.0	60.3	9.2
1960	24.5	8.4	15.4	51.7	10.0
1965	27.8	8.1	18.0	46.1	10.5
1970	23.7	10.9	22.5	42.9	10.8
1975	22.7	12.8	29.1	35.3	13.0
1978	21.6	15.6	33.8	28.9	14.4

SOURCES: U.S. Bureau of the Census, *Sixteenth Census of the United States: 1940*, "Characteristics by Age," vol. 4:1, U.S. Summary (Washington, D.C.: GPO, 1943), p. 30; *Census of Population: 1950*, "Marital Status," Special Reports, vol. 4:2, chapter D., p. 15; *Current Population Reports*, "Household and Family Characteristics: March 1978," series P-20, no. 340 (1979), Table E. Hereafter, all Census and Current Population Reports citations in this chapter will contain only titles, volume numbers, and dates of publication.

the trend in the percentage of all families (a subset of all households and excluding women living alone or with non-relatives) headed by women and the breakdown by type of family according to the marital status of the woman: spouse absent, never-married, divorced, or widowed. Since 1940 there has been a drop and then a rise in the proportion of all families headed by women and, more importantly, a large shift in the composition of the female headed families.

In 1940 a higher percentage of all families were headed by women (15.1 percent) than has been true at least through 1978 (the last year for which we have data). The female-headed family of 1940 was very different from today's stereotype of the separated, divorced, or un-married mother, struggling to bring up young children under the financial and emotional pressures of a poorly paying job or welfare. In 1940 and earlier, the female head of a family was much more likely to be a middle-aged widow who had one or more children living with her, or an older widow living with adult children or a sibling.[5] A higher fraction of never-married female heads in 1940 were more likely to be living with an adult relative than with a child. Thus the female-headed households in 1940 were more likely than today to include other adult non-family members who could contribute to the maintenance of the household.

The sharp decline from 1940 to the present in the fraction of female family heads who are widows has little to do with trends in mortality, but instead is related to trends in fertility and to living arrangements of widows. As discussed earlier, women in the older generation had fewer children—fully 44 percent of 70- to 74-year-olds in 1980 never had children or had only one child. While having fewer children gives these women less of an opportunity to head a family, they are more likely to head households. In addition, more widows with living children have chosen to live alone.

From 1940 to 1960, as the post-World War II surge in marriages in the middle generation increased the overall fraction of traditional husband/wife families, the fraction of all families headed by women fell by one-third. Simultaneously, the older generation's declining mortality rates increased its share of husband/wife families. Since 1960 the share of all families headed by women has been rising as an increasing number of never-married and divorced women with children have been setting up their own households. For example, among divorced women with one child in the 25- to 29-year age group, 49 percent lived with relatives in 1960 and 47 percent headed their own households. By 1975, 14 percent lived with relatives and 83 percent headed their own households. The remaining divorced mothers with one child (3 to 4 percent of the total) lived with a non-relative who was a household head, perhaps a partner or room-mate.

Two final interlocking features of Table 2.1 deserve comment. One is the rapid growth in the spouse-absent category before 1965 and the other is the similarly rapid increase in the divorced category since 1965. The liberalization of divorce laws after 1965 allowed separated spouse-absent couples, who had been building up in numbers during the 1960s, finally to divorce, accounting for the surge in divorces after that date.

The final category of female-headed *households* consists of single, divorced and separated women without children who, more than in the past, choose to live alone or head a household of non-family individuals. By examining changes in household size, we can better understand these trends.

Decline in Household Size and the Rise of Solo Living

The decline in household size and the formation of additional households can be inferred from Figures 2.1 and 2.2 by the increase in the number of household heads and the reduction in the number of children and others within households. The persistent decline in

Table 2.2.   Household Sizes, 1790–1978

Year	Number of Households (1,000s)	Distribution of Household Sizes (Percentages)					
		1 person	*2 persons*	*3 persons*	*4 persons*	*5+ persons*	*Mean Size*
1790	558	3.7	7.8	11.7	13.8	62.9	5.79
1900	15,946	5.1	15.0	17.6	16.9	45.5	4.76
1940	34,949	7.1	24.8	22.4	18.1	27.6	3.67
1950	43,468	10.9	28.8	22.6	17.8	20.0	3.37
1960	52,610	13.1	27.8	18.9	17.6	22.6	3.33
1970	62,874	17.0	28.8	17.3	15.8	21.1	3.14
1975	71,120	19.6	30.6	17.4	15.6	16.8	2.94
1978	76,030	22.0	30.7	17.2	15.7	14.5	2.81

SOURCES: *Current Population Reports,* "Households and Families by Type: March 1978," series P-20, no. 340 (1979), Table B; U.S. Bureau of the Census, *Historical Statistics of the United States, Colonial Times to 1970,* Part 1 (1975), pp. 41–42.

percentage of large households since 1790 and the recent increase in one- and two-person households is detailed in Table 2.2. Before 1940 the shrinking of household size was due primarily to a drop in the proportion of households with 5 or more people. Those large households fell from 62 percent of all households in 1790 to 28 percent in 1940. Since 1940 the average household size has continued to decrease not only because of the continued decline in large households but also because of the increase in one- and two-person households.[6] Even during the post-war baby boom, the growing proportion of couples with four or more children did not match the rapid increase in one- and two-person households, and average household size continued to shrink.

The initial decline in large households was caused by fewer families with a large number of children and fewer households containing non-nuclear family members. The post-1940 increase in small households is primarily due to a rise in the number of empty-nest households (particularly for the middle generation), the number of widows who live alone (particularly the older generation), and the number of single, divorced, and separated people (primarily in the younger generation) who head their own households. The increase in the number of one-person households is a dramatic departure from most of our historical experience; traditionally, adults have lived in households with other adults.

The middle generation contributes less to single-person households and more to two- and three-person households, because most of its members are still married and because the divorced and separated women still have children living at home. In the 1950s and 1960s, even those divorced and separated without children were less prone to head their own households and instead lived with relatives. Quick remarriage in this group, especially for men, narrowed the opportunity to live alone, and the women who lived with relatives expected the arrangement to be temporary until they remarried. Today a higher fraction of the middle generation's divorced and separated maintain independent households, and thereby contribute somewhat to small households.

The younger generation, born after 1940, is a large contributor to single-person households. Both never-married and divorced people in this group more often prefer to live alone than their counterparts in earlier generations. The proportion of never-married males and females in their 20s heading their own households more than doubled between 1960 and 1975, and most of these individuals lived alone. Also, among divorced women 25–29 years old who were childless in 1960, fully 59 percent moved back in with relatives and only 28 percent headed their own household. By 1975 the fraction of the 25- to 29-year-old group who moved back with relatives fell to 23 percent, and heads of household increased to 53 percent. Those of this group who lived with non-relatives rose from 13 percent in 1960 to 24 percent in 1975.[7]

The changes in household size can be summarized simply by noting that during this century the fraction of one- and two-person households has grown from 20 percent to over 50 percent of the total; three- and four-person households have held a constant share of about 35 percent of the total; and large households of five or more dropped from over 45 to under 15 percent of the total. All three adult generations contributed to the decline in household size, with the youngest and oldest contributing the most and with the oldest contributing at all stages of its life course.

When population grows and household size declines as much as it has in the United States, a rapid increase in the number of households and families results, with great diversity in age structure, sex ratio, marital status, presence of children, and a host of other social and economic characteristics of these households. The projected delayed marriage, lower fertility, higher divorce, and increasing number of empty-nest households will heighten these trends.

Decline in Husband/Wife Households

The most striking change that has taken place in the over-all structure of American households is the decline in the share headed by a married couple. Of the new households formed each year from 1950 to 1970, half or more were headed by a married couple. Since 1970, however, male-headed and female-headed families and households made up of unrelated individuals have increased dramatically. Between 1975 and 1979, over 6 million households were added in the United States. Almost 70 percent of these were households headed by a male or female not living in a nuclear family; only 11.5 percent were headed by a married couple (Table 2.3).[8] During the last two years of this period, between 1977 and 1979, the rate of formation of new husband/wife households had fallen still further, with only 6 percent of the 3 million new households headed by married couples.[9]

Adults who are today in the prime marriage ages (those born between 1940 and 1960 and age 20 to 40 in 1980) almost equal the total number of all other adults in the population. Potentially, they could bring about a tremendous surge in marriage and family building. But they are just barely replacing those married-couple households in all three generations that are being broken up by death or divorce. The over-all fraction of U.S. households headed by two spouses peaked in 1949 at 79 percent. Today, it has dropped to 61 percent.

The baby boom generation is responsible for a good deal of the decline in the share of husband/wife households, but only since 1960, when its first members reached their adult years. Even before then,

Table 2.3.   **Components of Household Increase, 1950–1979**

Years	Total Net Increase in Households (1,000s)	Percentage of Total Increase		
		Husband/ Wife	Other Families	Unrelated Individual
1950–1955	4,320	50.4	6.2	43.2
1955–1960	4,925	61.0	3.4	35.6
1960–1965	4,637	52.5	10.8	37.6
1965–1970	5,965	50.9	9.9	39.3
1970–1975	7,719	28.8	24.4	46.8
1975–1979	6,210	11.5	19.7	68.8

SOURCE: *Current Population Reports*, "Households and Families by Type: March 1979 (Advance Report)," series P-20, no. 345 (1979), Table 3.

as many as 40 to 50 percent of all the households formed by the middle and older generations were "other families" and "unrelated individuals."

The drop in the share of husband/wife households is plotted in Figure 2.3. Uppermost in the figure is the ratio of husband/wife couples to all unrelated individuals who head households. A decline in this ratio can be caused either by a relatively greater number of unrelated individuals compared to married couples in the household population or by their increasing propensity to head households—or, of course, by a combination of the two trends. The middle line is a ratio of husband/wife couples to unrelated individuals living in, but not necessarily heads of, households. It is an indicator of the trend in the relative number of potential unrelated household heads. The lowermost trend line gives the ratio of female to male unrelated individuals. This ratio is particularly sensitive to the relative fraction of unrelated individuals who are widows and who head their own households.

The uppermost line—the trend in the ratio of husband/wife to unrelated individual house heads—shows a sharp and steady decline throughout the period covered. In 1948 a household was eight times more likely to be headed by a married couple than by an unrelated individual. By 1979 only two-and-a-half times more households were headed by married couples than by unrelated individuals. The initial drop in the ratio, between 1947 and 1965, had nothing to do with the life style of the younger generation since it had not yet reached adulthood. Part of the decline in this period was caused by women in the older generation who increasingly outlived their husbands and decided not to live with relatives after they were widowed. Part of the decline can be accounted for by members of the middle generation who maintained their own households instead of returning home during the spans of their lives when they were not married. This initial period did not see a big change in the relative numbers of husband/wife couples to unrelated individuals living in, but not necessarily heads of, households (middle trend). The ratio moved slowly from about 4.1 to 3.5 between 1947 and 1965, indicating that it was not an increase in the numbers of unrelated individuals but their increasingly independent living arrangements that played a major role in the initial decline of households headed by married couples. The lowermost trend line shows that from 1947 to about 1967 the ratio of female to male unrelated individuals in households was on the

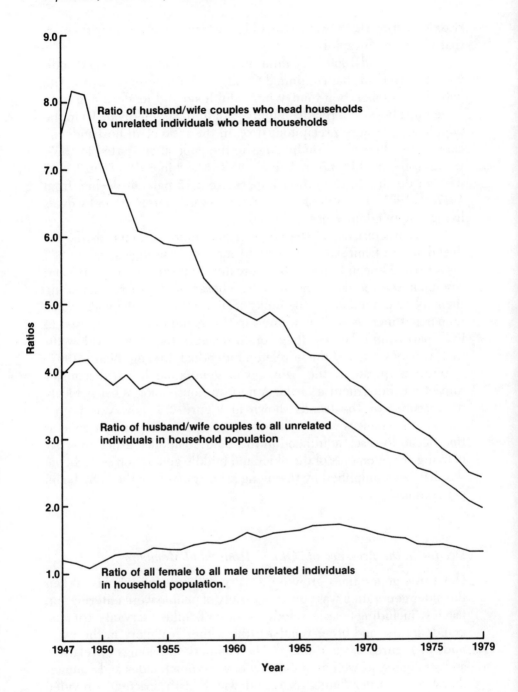

Figure 2.3. Husband/Wife Couples and Unrelated Individuals, 1947–1979. *(Source: Appendix Table B. 3.)*

rise, indicating that it was *women's* living arrangements, in particular, that changed so rapidly.

Since the mid-1960s the ratio of husband/wife to unrelated individual households has continued to fall, but for different reasons. The baby boom generation's entry into adulthood and its declining marriage rates boost the relative numbers of unrelated individuals in the population. A more precipitous drop in the ratio of all husband/wife couples to all unrelated individuals in the population started in 1965, going from roughly 3.5 to 1 to about 1.9 to 1 in 1979. That is a 42 percent decline in the ratio compared to a 12 percent decline from 1947 to 1965. In addition, the trend toward unrelated individuals living independently has persisted.

Two characteristics of the younger generation account for the reduced ratio of unrelated women to men in households since 1967 (lower trend line in Figure 2.3). A greater proportion of both men and women in the younger generation has chosen not to marry, increasing their relative numbers in the ranks of all unrelated individuals. Since unmarried men as well as women in this generation have chosen to live apart from relatives, they counterbalance the female-widow tilt that heavily weighted the unrelated individual category before 1967.

Without question, the baby boom generation has had a major impact on the structure of the American household. What is nicely underscored by the trends shown in Figure 2.3, however, is that some of the changes were well under way before the younger generation began to reach adulthood in the 1960s. The increasing diversity of living arrangements of the older and middle generation set a theme that has been amplified by the living arrangements of the baby boom generation.

Decline in the Presence of "Other" Household Members

Our three generations grew up in very different households. When the older generation was young, a variety of people were entering and leaving, including boarders, lodgers, other families, servants, friends, grandparents, and other relatives (the "other" category in the pyramids of Figures 2.1 and 2.2).[10] The comings and goings of relatives and strangers, as well as siblings who were much older and younger (because of larger family sizes and wider birth spacing), provided varied and direct contacts with people in different life stages. The age structure of the household was much more heterogeneous than today's. Infants, adolescents, single adults, middle-aged parents, and older relatives were much more likely to be present on any given day.

The middle generation had fewer siblings on the average, but aunts, uncles, and cousins—particularly those who were unmarried or childless—joined their households from time to time. Even though the 1940 pyramid shows the greater evidence of presence of "others" than years later, by that time the majority of the "extended" household members were relatives.

By 1970 very few people who did not live alone lived with someone other than their spouse or their children. The households in which the younger generation grew up had become standardized to include one to three siblings (two to four years different in age), two parents (approximately 25 years older), and no one else.

The younger generation has continued the process of paring down household structure in their own lives and in the lives of their children. More and more people of this generation live, by choice, in single-person households, and more of this generation's children are being raised in single-parent households. The children in both two-parent and one-parent households have fewer siblings.

Although these changes point to a further simplification of household structure, there are simultaneously counterbalancing trends. People of the younger generation who may live alone at one time live at other times with a greater variety of temporary roommates and live-in boyfriends and girlfriends. They also have more diverse temporary living arrangements because of moving, changing jobs, or attending school. Single parents, too, are more inclined than in the past to share their households, at least temporarily, with friends and partners.

Today's marriages increasingly involve a remarriage for at least one of the partners, so that the growing number of children involved in these remarriages interact with two living parents and one or more step parents.[11] Not only are there fewer children per household, but at the same time, children are increasingly members of more than one household. Finally, the greater number of mothers who are in the paid labor force have introduced young children to a variety of caretakers, including relatives, babysitters, and those who conduct play groups, day-care, and after-school programs.

The net effect of these countervailing changes—the paring down of basic household size and structure while increasing the opportunities for more interaction with others *outside* the household—places the younger generation in stark contrast to their parents' generation, whose family structure was static by comparison, and it separates them from their grandparents' generation, who experienced the interaction with a variety of others from *within* larger households.

Life-Course Variables

Life-course variables—particularly marital status, fertility, and the extent to which unattached adults live independently—determine household composition. Because we are interested in the most probable changes in household structure over the next decade, we will examine in greater detail the trends in these three variables, with an eye to predicting their future change. (These analyses and projections, which we will briefly summarize, are an ongoing activity at the Joint Center for Urban Studies.)

Our projections of life-course variables are based on the method of analysis that traces the actual experience of succeeding age groupings (birth cohorts) as their members marry, have children, divorce, are widowed, and choose living arrangements. The strength of cohort analysis is that age groupings establish distinctive patterns of inertia and of change so that one can project patterns *within* each cohort. In addition, trends in the experience of successive birth cohorts establish an over-all pattern of change that allows one to better understand and project life-course trends for specific ages over time.

Marital Status

For our purposes, we distinquish among four marital status categories: (1) never-married; (2) currently married with spouse present; (3) separated/divorced or spouse absent; and (4) widowed. Only the never-married category is a pure type in the sense that people in this category have always been "never married." As the cohort ages, the proportion never-married can move in only one direction, downward.

All other categories receive members with a variety of previous marital histories, and as the cohort ages, the proportion in any one category can increase or decrease. The "currently married" includes men and women married one or more times. Its size depends on trends in first marriages and remarriages and on trends in separation, divorce, and widowhood. Even the widowed proportion can change unevenly over time, depending on mortality and remarriage trends. Because three of the marital status categories—the currently married, the separated/divorced or spouse absent and the widowed—are subject to a number of influences that can add to and subtract from their size, we limited our examination of cohort trajectories to *net* changes in these categories. Only in the never-married categories can gross flows in one direction be examined.

The Never-Married. One difference among the three generations is in the proportion still single while in the young adult years. Figure 2.4 plots trends in the proportion never-married in four five-year age groups, beginning at age 15 and ending at age 34, from 1890 to 1990. Most members of the older generation (born before 1920) had passed through their young adult years by 1945. For both men and women this period marked a gradual decline in the proportion never-married, except for a slight rise during the 1930s Depression.

The marriage pattern of the middle generation established itself between 1945 and 1965 when those born between 1920 and 1940 entered and passed through their early adult years. This was a period of greatly accelerated marriages and sharp declines in never-marrieds.

The younger generation, those born since 1940, began to enter young adulthood in the 1960s and 1970s, a period of delay in marriage. By 1978 the increasing proportion of never-marrieds in the younger generation returned the never-married population to levels in line with the pre-1940 trend, but the rate of increase in the proportion single for specific age groups from one year to the next was greater than ever before experienced by any successive cohorts born in the twentieth century. We have projected a continued increase in the proportion never-married through 1990 based upon present trends. If this trajectory materializes, the 1990 levels of proportion never-married will be the highest ever in this century.

Several related variables argue in favor of a continued upswing in the proportion single through the 1980s. Men, who traditionally have preferred to marry women a few years younger than themselves, will find a growing shortage of younger women (indicated by the tapering of the bottom of the population pyramid in Figures 2.1 and 2.2). This change in age structure will put a "marriage squeeze" on men, forcing them to delay marriage until they consider women from a wider age range—younger and older—to be desirable marriage partners. Men who are facing a shortage of women of the "right" age might put pressure on women to marry younger, and this could create a reversal in the trend toward delayed marriage *for women*. However, women's rising education levels and labor force participation, declining child-

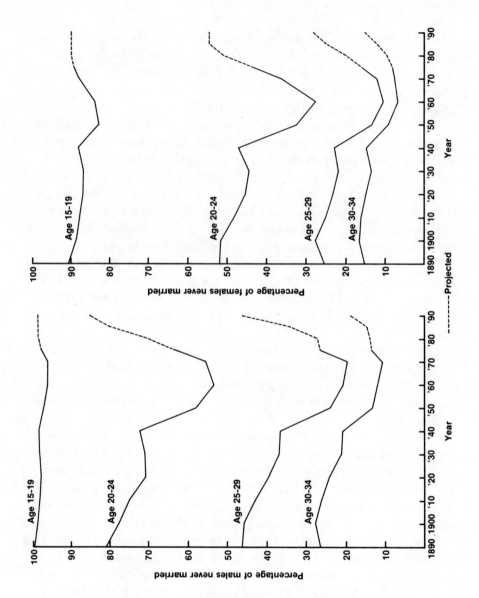

Figure 2.4. Percentage of Population Never-Married, 1890–1990. (*Source: Appendix Table B.4.*)

bearing aspirations, and the increasing desire to first establish identities other than that of wife and mother provide strong reasons to expect a continuation of delayed marriage for women as well as men.

Table 2.4 presents observations and extrapolations for selected cohorts of women from each generation, giving the percentage never-married during each year of their 20s, as well as the average time spent never-married during each half of that life-course decade. Similar information for all other cohorts born between 1901 and 1960 is given in Appendix Table B.5. Table 2.4 shows how the middle generation differed from the older and the younger generations by spending much less time being single, especially in its early 20s. We project that those born 1955–1960 will surpass the older groups in the amount of time never-married when they are in their early 20s.

The Divorced. Once an individual marries, the proportion of time spent being married depends on the chances of divorce and widowhood, and on the likelihood of remarriage. While trends in divorce

Table 2.4. Never-Married Women Age 20–29

| | Generation and Year of Birth | | | | | | |
| | Older Generation | | Middle Generation | | Younger Generation | | |
Age	1910	1920	1930	1940	1945	1950	1955
	Percentage Unmarried during Twenties						
20	60.5	62.8	50.0	45.8	51.3	56.7	(62.4)
21	53.0	52.8	38.3	36.0	40.7	(46.0)	(53.8)
22	45.2	43.0	29.2	27.1	30.3	(36.0)	(45.4)
23	38.3	34.3	22.6	21.0	23.6	(30.1)	(39.3)
24	32.6	27.7	18.1	17.3	19.5	(25.9)	(33.5)
25	28.5	22.6	14.8	14.7	16.2	(22.4)	(28.5)
26	24.7	19.0	12.9	12.5	(14.2)	(19.4)	—
27	21.6	15.5	10.7	11.0	(13.1)	(17.4)	—
28	19.8	13.3	9.8	10.1	(12.5)	(16.1)	—
29	17.5	11.1	8.9	9.2	(12.0)	(15.3)	—
	Mean Percentage of Time Unmarried during Twenties						
20–24	45.9	44.1	31.6	29.4	33.1	38.9	46.9
25–29	22.4	16.3	11.4	11.5	13.6	18.1	—

NOTE: Parentheses indicate projected values. All other values are based upon interpolations between decennial censuses. See Appendix Table B.5 for data on all other cohorts of women born between 1901 and 1960; for methodology used to derive interpolated values, see Dowell Myers, "The Housing Progress of Young Cohorts" (Ph.D. dissertation, The Massachusetts Institute of Technology, 1980), Chapter 5.

and widowhood have been consistent enough to allow us to make projections of the chances that a marriage will be *broken* by death or divorce, remarriage trends have been far less predictable, making projections a bit risky. A continued increase in divorce rates would have little impact on the proportions currently divorced *if* remarriage rates kept pace. If, on the other hand, remarriage rates slow down while divorce rates increase, as has been the case during the mid-1970s, the proportion currently divorced increases rapidly.

The fact that divorce levels have continued to rise since 1975 can be seen in Table 2.5, which presents the percentage of the currently divorced out of *all women* (including the never-married) in each age group for selected years. While it is not appropriate to use such a percentage to project divorce levels into the future because of the influence of the never-married trends, Table 2.5 does show how divorce levels have risen across all age groups in recent years.

After examining trends in the proportion of the ever-married who are currently divorced or separated (see Figure 2.5 and Appendix Table B.6), we project that proportions currently divorced will increase at a moderate pace for women over the next decade and at a slightly accelerated pace for men.

The Widowed. Mortality trends profoundly influence household composition. First, the overall decline in death rates has meant that spouses live together for a longer period into the empty-nest stage. Second, the more rapid increase in women's life expectancy has meant a steady rise in the ratio of male/female mortality and a steady decline in the sex ratio of males to females in the older age groupings (see Table 2.6 and Figure 2.6).

Table 2.5.   Percentage of Women Currently Divorced, 1950–1978

| | *Age of Women* | | | | | | |
Year	*20–24*	*25–29*	*30–34*	*35–44*	*45–54*	*55–64*	*65–74*
1950	1.4	2.6	2.6	3.4	2.9	2.1	0.9
1955	1.4	2.2	2.8	3.8	3.3	2.4	1.4
1960	1.7	2.5	3.1	3.8	3.9	3.1	1.7
1965	2.0	3.4	3.3	4.4	4.6	3.9	2.3
1970	2.2	4.1	4.7	5.3	5.1	4.4	2.9
1975	3.3	6.7	7.3	7.7	6.9	5.5	3.3
1978	3.6	8.1	10.5	10.2	7.9	6.4	3.9

SOURCE: Various issues of *Current Population Reports*, "Marital Status and Living Arrangements," series P-20. Data for all years except 1978 are three-year averages around pivotal date.

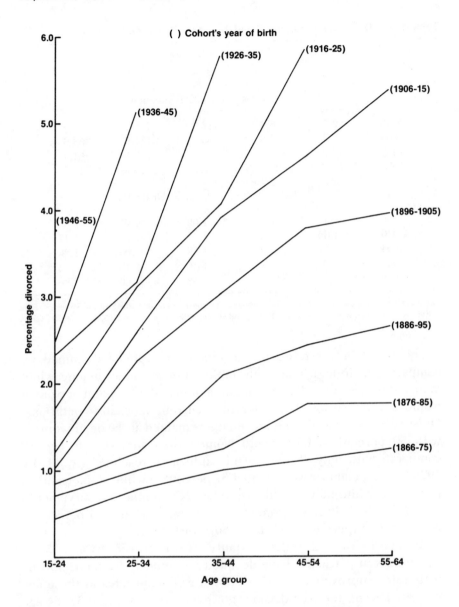

Figure 2.5. Divorced Women as Percentage of Those Ever-Married, 1866–1875 to 1946–1955 Birth Cohorts. *(Source: Appendix Table B.6.)*

Table 2.6. Death Rates for the Population Age 55 and Older, 1940–1977

Year	Age Groups				
	55–64	65–74	75–84	85+	65+
Rates per 1,000 Population					
1940	22.2	48.4	112.0	235.7	72.2
1954	17.4	37.9	86.0	181.6	58.6
1968	17.0	37.2	82.9	195.8	61.4
1977	14.3	30.5	71.5	145.9	52.6
Ratio of Male to Female Death Rates					
1900	1.14	1.11	1.08	1.05	1.06
1940	1.45	1.29	1.17	1.08	1.17
1954	1.82	1.57	1.29	1.06	1.30
1968	2.07	1.88	1.46	1.18	1.44
1976	1.99	1.97	1.58	1.26	1.46

SOURCE: _Current Population Reports_, Special Studies, "Prospective Trends in the Size and Structure of the Elderly Population, Impact of Mortality Trends, and Some Implications," series P-23, no. 78 (1979), Tables 6–7.

The trend in sex ratios in the older ages can be examined by comparing male and female life tables. For example, among white men and women in 1940, 58 percent of men and 69 percent of women would survive to age 65 under then-current mortality conditions. Once reaching age 65, the advantage remained in favor of women, with 50 percent of 65-year-old women then surviving to age 80 compared with only 38 percent of white men reaching age 80. By 1974 life expectancy rose such that 82 percent of white women and 68 percent of white men would live to age 65. Among the survivors to age 65 in 1974, fully 61 percent of women, but only 40 percent of men, could expect to reach their 80th birthday.[12]

As seen in Table 2.6, the mortality rates in the 55–64 and 65–74 age groups in particular have declined less quickly for men, putting male rates approximately twice as high as female rates in those age groups. During the past decade, however, women in the 55–64 age group have lost some of their advantage, not because of higher female death rates, but because of a rapidly lowering of male mortality, particularly among men 55–64. Taking into account declining rates of mortality and the slowdown in the divergence of male and female mortality rates over the age of 55, our analysis of proportion of ever-married men and women in each age group who are currently widowed showed only a small decline in recent years for the population

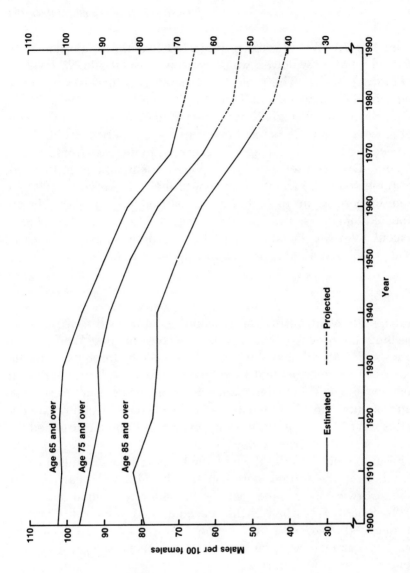

Figure 2.6. Sex Ratios in the Older Ages, 1900–1990. (*Source: U.S. Bureau of the Census, Current Population Reports, "Demographic Aspects of Aging and the Older Population in the United States," series P-23, no. 59, May 1976*)

under age 70. We, therefore, projected that the proportion ever-married who are widowed would remain constant at 1975 levels.

Future Trends. The projections show sharp increases in never-married men and women in their 20s between 1975 and 1990. Never-married women aged 25–29 are expected to increase from 16 percent of the age group to 28 percent over this 15-year period, while never-married men of the same age are expected to increase from 26 to 46 percent. Divorced/separated and spouse-absent women in their 30s are projected to be about 20 percent of their age group by 1990, up from 13 percent in 1975. Formerly married men in their 30s are expected to increase from the 1975 range of 7 to 9 percent to 14 to 15 percent by 1990. Detailed marital status projections for the years 1980, 1985, and 1990 are given in Appendix B.7.

Fertility

Perhaps no event during the twentieth century will have such far-reaching consequences for American society as the post-World War II baby boom. It will have an impact on society throughout its life course. Many changes that have taken place since World War II in such areas as housing, nutrition, education, work, health care, and entertainment, in addition to household and family structure, are due to this wave of population sweeping over institutions accustomed to a smaller and more orderly flow.[13]

From the mid-1950s to the mid-1960s, more than 42 million babies were born in the United States—better than 4.2 million a year. This is almost twice the number born to the older generation during the 1930s. Since 1961, when births peaked at 4.35 million, the number has declined. A low of 3.1 million births was reached in 1975 and the total has remained between 3.1 and 3.4 million a year ever since. This trend is plotted in Figure 2.7.

The fertility distribution of the three generations can be seen in Table 2.7. The middle generation, whose childbearing was essentially completed by 1975, had between 2.8 and 3.2 births per woman—significantly more than the older generation (except for the very oldest). The younger generation has embarked on a trend that may place their fertility even below that of the older generation.

Table 2.7 also points out a basic difference in the distribution of family size between the middle and older generations. The range of four family sizes (0, 1, 2–3, and 4 or more children ever born) is fairly evenly distributed across the older generation. By contrast, in the

Figure 2.7. Annual Number of Births, 1929–1978. (*Source: Appendix Table B. 8.*)

Table 2.7.   Cumulative Fertility and Distribution of Women by Number of Births, 1975

Age	Total Births per Woman	Percentage of Women by Number of Births			
		0	*1*	*2–3*	*4+*
Younger Generation (Cohorts born 1941–1960)					
15–19	0.0863	92.6	6.4	1.0	0.0
20–24	0.5597	62.5	23.3	13.5	0.7
25–29	1.3692	31.1	25.4	38.0	5.5
30–34	2.2122	15.2	16.2	51.5	17.1
Middle Generation (Cohorts born 1921–1940)					
35–39	2.8799	9.6	11.1	48.3	31.0
40–44	3.1901	8.8	9.7	44.3	33.7
45–49	3.0787	10.6	11.4	43.6	34.4
50–54	2.8042	10.6	14.4	44.6	30.4
Older Generation (Cohorts born 1920 and before)					
55–59	2.5740	13.9	17.4	43.3	25.4
60–64	2.3543	18.2	20.4	39.7	21.7
65–69	2.2858	21.4	22.2	35.6	20.8
70–74	2.4414	20.0	23.0	33.7	22.9
75–70	2.6759	19.7	20.6	33.2	26.5
80–84	2.9326	19.1	17.9	32.2	31.8
85+	3.1368	21.0	15.0	28.0	36.0

SOURCE: Robert L. Heuser, *Fertility Tables for Birth Cohorts by Color*, DHEW Publication no. (HRA)76-1152 (Rockville, Md.: National Center for Health Statistics, 1976). Additional data for period 1975–1977 provided by NCHS.

middle generation only about one-fifth are childless or parents of an only child and four-fifths have two or more children. The 2-to-3 child category gains prominence as one moves from older to younger within the middle generation. The younger generation is continuing this preference for 2 to 3 children with over half expecting to bear that many.

Figures 2.8, 2.9, and 2.10 give further insight into the direction of family size for the younger generation. Slightly over 50 percent of the older women in that generation (born between 1941 and 1945) will have 2 or 3 children by age 35 (Figure 2.8). The younger members (those born between 1950 and 1953) will not reach that level unless they accelerate their childbearing in their late 20s and early 30s. At all ages, the younger generation appears to be heading toward higher

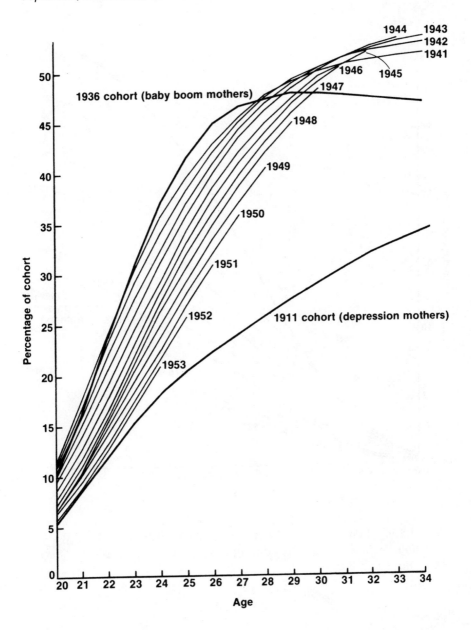

Figure 2.8. Percentage of Cohorts Born since 1940 of All U.S. Women with Two or Three Live Births during Prime Reproductive Years. (*Source: Appendix Table B. 9.*)

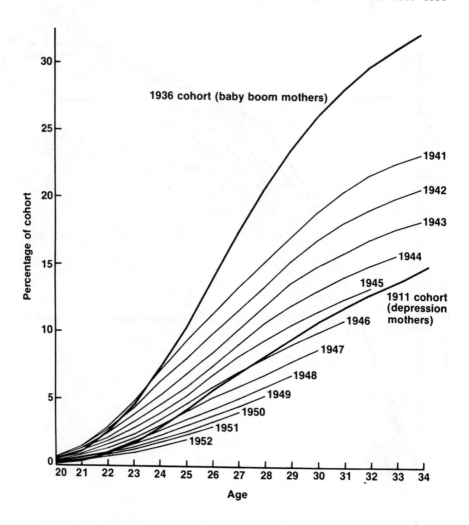

Figure 2.9. Percentage of Cohorts Born since 1940 of All U.S. Women with Four or More Live Births during Prime Reproductive Years. *(Source: Appendix Table B.9.)*

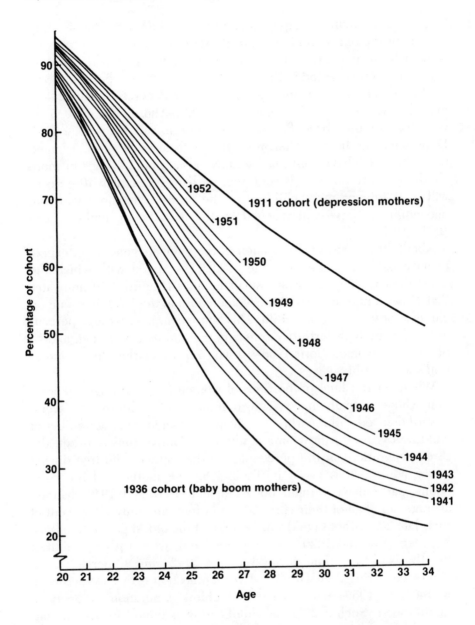

Figure 2.10. Percentage of Cohorts Born since 1940 of All U.S. Women with Zero or One Live Birth during Prime Reproductive Years. (*Source: Appendix Table B. 9.*)

levels of 2- to 3-child completed families than either the low-fertility cohorts in the oldest generation (represented in the three figures by women born in 1911) or the high-fertility cohorts from the middle generation (represented in the three figures by women born in 1936).

The percentage of women of the younger generation having 4 or more births is steadily dropping (Figure 2.9). Those born in 1945 (32 years old in the three figures) are about to fall below the 1911 Depression mothers in the proportion with large families. Women born after 1945 have continued to move away from having 4 or more children. If present trends continue, perhaps fewer than 10 percent will have four or more children in the future, compared with the maximum of 37 percent reached by the baby boom mothers born 1931–1935.

About 20 percent of the women in the younger generation expect to have only one child or none at all. The speed with which the generation is moving toward small families (Figure 2.10) indicates that 40 percent or more of these women born in the 1950s may end up childless or with only one child. This figure compares with 20 percent or less for the high-fertility mothers of the middle generation, and 43 percent for women born 1906–10 who represent the older generation's low fertility.

Whatever the final proportions of women in the younger generation who eventually have a given number of children, the trend toward delayed childbearing has given them an increasing number of child-free years during young adulthood. Comparisons between the three generations in the percentage of time spent child-free during young adulthood is given in Table 2.8. The mothers of the baby boom, particularly women born between 1931 and 1940, had on average only half of their early 20s child-free, and only 20 percent of their late 20s without children. Women of the oldest generation born between 1911 and 1920, on the other hand, were without children two-thirds of their time during the ages 20–24 and 40 percent were child-free during their late 20s. Every indication is that women born in the late 1950s will surpass the oldest generation in delaying motherhood. Such a delay in childbearing is bound to have a considerable and continuing impact on the living arrangements, labor force experiences, and life styles of the younger generation.

Household Headship

We seem to be rapidly approaching the time when the vast majority of adults, regardless of age, sex or marital status, will head their own

Table 2.8.   Child-Free Women Age 20–29, 1901–1955 Birth Cohorts

	Birth Cohorts						
	Older Generation		*Middle Generation*		*Younger Generation*		
Age	*1901– 1910*	*1911– 1920*	*1921– 1930*	*1931– 1940*	*1941– 1945*	*1946– 1950*	*1951– 1955*
	Percentage Child-Free during Twenties						
20	76.6	79.7	77.3	69.0	69.6	73.6	75.1
21	68.7	73.0	68.3	58.1	59.6	64.6	68.2
22	61.7	66.5	59.3	48.1	50.6	56.3	62.2
23	55.4	60.2	50.8	39.4	43.0	49.3	56.3[a]
24	49.9	54.2	43.1	32.2	36.6	43.3	50.6[a]
25	45.3	48.8	36.4	26.6	31.4	38.2	—
26	41.3	43.9	30.7	22.4	27.0	34.0	—
27	38.0	39.3	26.1	19.2	23.5	30.4	—
28	35.2	35.2	22.6	16.8	20.7	26.4[b]	—
29	32.7	31.7	19.8	15.0	18.7	23.1[b]	—
	Percentage of Age Period Spent Child-Free						
20–24	62.5	66.7	59.8	49.4	51.9	57.4	62.5[a]
25–29	38.5	39.8	27.1	20.0	24.3	30.4	—
20–29	50.5	53.3	43.4	34.7	38.1	43.9	—

SOURCE: Same as Table 2.7.

[a] Based on partial information for 1954 and 1955 cohorts.
[b] Based on partial information for 1949 and 1950 cohorts.

households. A brief explanation of the general implications of "headship" may be useful since it is neither so straightforward nor in such common usage as our other two categories, marital status and fertility.

A household, described earlier, is made up of one or more people who occupy a housing unit, whether or not they are related. In examining headship, we will be looking at the proportion of adults among certain population groupings (husband/wife couples, unmarried adults, and so on) who are the principal adults in the household. A low headship rate in any adult group necessarily implies that a good many people within that group are living in households headed by someone else, or in group quarters (units containing five or more unrelated individuals), or in institutions. For example, a low headship rate for husband/wife couples of a certain age means that a high proportion are not living independently, but are doubled up in other households. A high headship rate for this same group of husband/wife couples means they head their own households, but they may or may not have other unmarried adults living with them. As we saw earlier (Figures 2.1 and 2.2), very few households in recent years have other adults present.

Table 2.9 presents data on the proportion of all husband/wife couples in the total population (by age of husband) who headed their own households from 1930 to 1970. As can be seen, this proportion is generally high at all ages and all dates. By 1970 only young couples, where the husband was in his early 20s, had levels below 90 percent. Over time, headship rates increase for all age groups, with the very young and very old experiencing the largest gains. Headship rates of husband/wife couples fell slightly between 1930 and 1940, during the Depression. The lowest rate of any group in that period was 68 percent for 20- to 24-year-old husbands.

In contrast to the generally high headship rates of husband/wife couples are the much lower rates for unmarried adults (Table 2.10). This pattern has been changing rapidly in recent years, however, with large increases in the headship rates for young unmarried adults. For example, among unmarried males age 30–34, only 14.3 percent headed their own household in 1930. This figure grew to only 16.4 percent in 1940 and 19.6 percent in 1950, but then jumped to 34.1 percent by 1960. By 1970 the headship rate for these unmarried males had topped 50 percent. Similar sharp increases in unmarried

Table 2.9.   **Proportion of Husband/Wife Couples Heading Their Own Households, 1930–1970**

Age of Husband	Year				
	1930	1940	1950	1960	1970
20–24	.7150	.6821	.7144	.7972	.8273
25–29	.8365	.8157	.8346	.9096	.9267
30–34	.8917	.8697	.8830	.9345	.9436
35–44	.9257	.9044	.9088	.9455	.9520
45–54	.9377	.9178	.9193	.9481	.9562
55–64	.9349	.9208	.9226	.9440	.9491
65–74	.9100	.9000	.9049	.9336	.9432
75+	.8376	.8415	.8559	.8909	.9065

Source: Calculated from data contained in *Census of Population*, various "Special Reports," 1930–1970.
Note: Population data refer to total resident population, not just household population.

Table 2.10. Proportion of Unmarried Adults Heading Their Own Households, 1930–1970

Age and Sex	Year				
	1930	1940	1950	1960	1970
Males					
20–24	.0386	.0333	.0437	.0812	.1512
25–29	.0754	.0834	.1109	.2133	.3859
30–34	.1435	.1646	.1960	.3415	.5226
35–44	.2660	.3059	.3349	.4788	.6484
45–54	.4319	.4719	.4868	.6108	.7715
55–64	.5168	.5636	.5437	.6632	.8095
65–74	.4972	.5661	.5459	.6671	.7830
75 +	.3834	.4542	.4428	.5267	.6235
Females					
20–24	.0439	.0452	.0811	.1956	.2721
25–29	.1212	.1363	.2221	.4557	.6474
30–34	.2491	.2893	.3785	.6604	.8401
35–44	.4375	.5227	.5509	.7696	.9152
45–54	.5579	.6415	.6480	.7632	.8762
55–64	.5487	.6080	.6071	.7073	.8173
65–74	.4718	.5426	.5494	.6527	.7609
75 +	.3395	.4170	.4158	.4862	.5695

SOURCE: Calculated from data contained in *Census of Population*, various "Special Reports," 1930–1970.

NOTE: "Unmarried adults" category includes never-married, divorced and widowed. Population data refer to total resident population, not just household population.

headship rates occurred in other age groups for both men and women.

The headship rates for unmarried women are generally higher than for men, particularly in the younger age groups. This is because more young unmarried men than women reside in group quarters, institutions, and barracks. Headship rates for unmarried women have increased so rapidly since 1950 that by 1970 the proportion in the middle adult years heading households approached the levels for married couples. Unmarried women age 25–29 and 30–34 in 1970 had increased their headship three to five times over the 1930 level.

A breakdown of the population in greater detail on age and marital status, and with the addition of the number of children under the age of 15 present in the household, appears in Table 2.11 for the years 1960, 1970, and 1975. Only selected population subgroups are reported in Table 2.11. Those not listed—for example, young married couples with children—generally have headship rates exceeding 98 percent all three years.

The biggest jump in headship rates has been for unmarried adults without children. This trend is even more significant than it appears because of the substantial growth in the number of these sorts of individuals. Increases have occurred in all categories in numbers of never-married men and women, divorced and separated men and

Table 2.11. Headship Rates for Selected Family Types, 1960, 1970, and 1975

	Year		
Age, Marital Status, and Children at Home	*1960*	*1970*	*1975*
20–24			
Male, Never-Married (0)[a]	.0802	.1507	.1889
Female, Never-Married (0)	.0894	.1499	.1866
Married Couples (0)	.9247	.9552	.9691
25–29			
Male, Never-Married (0)	.1869	.3283	.4181
Female, Never-Married (0)	.1828	.3085	.4117
Married Couples (0)	.9451	.9707	.9775
30–34			
Female, Separated, Divorced, SA[b] (0)	.4339	.4308	.6419
Female, Separated, Divorced, SA (1)	.6303	.7895	.9060
Female, Separated, Divorced, SA (2 or 3)	.7556	.8816	.9400
Female, Separated, Divorced, SA (4+)	.8743	.9413	.9589
Married Couples (2 or 3)	.9888	.9956	.9957
35–39			
Female, Separated, Divorced, SA (0)	.5518	.5443	.7312
Female, Separated, Divorced, SA (1)	.7818	.8840	.9169
Female, Separated, Divorced, SA (2 or 3)	.8638	.9350	.9838
Female, Separated, Divorced, SA (4+)	.9363	.9692	.9769
Married Couples (2 or 3)	.9917	.9964	.9937
60–64			
Female, Widowed (0)	.7041	.8131	.8736
70–74			
Female, Widowed (0)	.6499	.7686	.8280
80–84			
Female, Widowed (0)	.5064	.7312	.7527

SOURCE: Joint Center tabulations of the 1960 and 1970 *Public Use Samples* and 1975 *Annual Housing Survey* tapes.

NOTE: Number of children under age 15 in parentheses.

[a] Because only people living in households are included in the calculation of the headship rates in Table 2.11, the rates are higher than those for similar groups in Tables 2.9 and 2.10 where individuals living outside of households were included in the denominator when calculating the rates.
[b] "Spouse Absent."

women without children, and women who are widowed in the empty-nest stage. Were it not for the large increases in headship rates among these population subgroups, the change in the structure of households and families that we observed in the first part of this section would not have been nearly so dramatic:

1. The number of households would have grown more slowly.
2. Household size would have decreased less rapidly.
3. More adult children would be living with their parents or siblings.
4. Husband/wife households would have continued to constitute most of the increase in new households.
5. Fewer people would be living alone.

Insufficient data exist to permit observation of complete patterns of headship trends over the life course of our three generations. We have estimated a 15-year segment (from 1960 to 1975) of the cohort life-course trajectories for headship by marital status and children ever born. As an example of this computation, trends for selected cohorts of never-marrieds are shown in Figure 2.11. The sharp rise in the rate of increase over the life course for younger members can be clearly seen. Furthermore, the trends from 1960 to 1975 are consistent enough to enable us to project with some confidence trends in household headship to 1990. Table 2.12 presents these projections of household headship for selected age, sex, and marital status categories experiencing the biggest changes between 1960 and 1975.[14]

Projections of Trends in Household and Family Structure to 1990

Our analysis and projections of trends in household and family structure were summarized in Chapter 1 and are presented here in greater detail in Table 2.13, and summarized in Table 2.14. The changes that have been taking place are discussed by focusing first on married-couple households, and then on households headed by men or women who are not married.

Married-Couple Households

Between 1960 and 1975, married-couple households increased by almost 8 million. Because the number of households headed by unmarried men and women grew even faster, however, the proportion of households headed by married couples fell from 74.8 percent

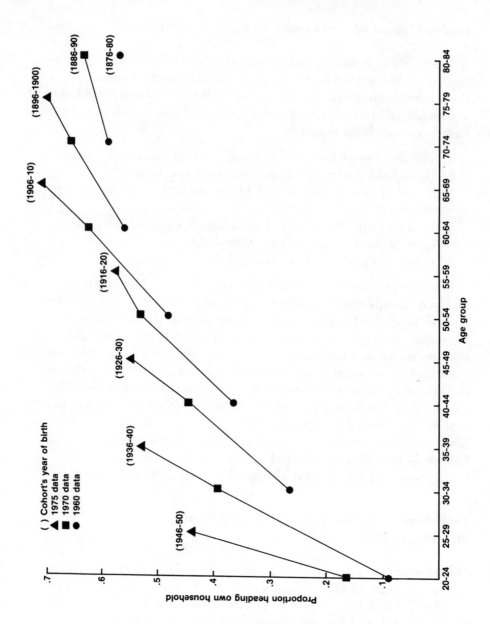

Figure 2.11. Cohort Trends in Headship Rates for Population Never-Married, 1960–1975, Alternate Five-Year Birth Cohorts. (*Source: Appendix Table B.10.*)

Table 2.12.   Trends in Headship Rates for Selected Age and Marital Status Categories, 1975 and 1990

Age and Marital Status	Year	
	1975	1990
Never-Married Men		
20–24	.2033	.2033
25–29	.4177	.4177
30–34	.4528	.5224
35–39	.5142	.6164
Never-Married Women		
20–24	.2502	.2662
25–29	.4636	.4901
30–34	.5637	.5582
35–39	.5512	.6007
Widowed Women		
60–64	.8762	.8660
65–69	.8548	.8701
70–74	.8305	.9169
75–79	.7882	.9094
Separated/Divorced Women		
25–29	.7592	.7398
30–34	.8632	.8382
35–39	.8857	.8557
40–44	.9076	.8637
45–49	.8723	.8932
50–54	.8398	.8999
55–59	.8524	.9229

SOURCE: See Appendix Table B.11.

to 65.4 percent of all households in that period. During the next 15-year period (1975 to 1990) we project the number of married-couple households to grow by only 3.5 million, and the total share of married-couple households to fall to 55 percent of all households.

Most of the increase in married-couple households between 1960 and 1975 was accounted for by couples who did not have any children under the age of 15 at home. Fully 90 percent of the new households were either young couples who were postponing childbearing or empty-nest couples whose youngest child was 15 or older. Between 1975 and 1990 only about 41 percent of the projected increase in married-couple households will be childless households, because the baby boom generation will be entering the marriage and childbearing years during this period. By 1990 roughly half of all married couples will have children under 15 in the household, but this represents only

Table 2.13. Types of Households in 1960, 1970, and 1975 and Projected for 1980, 1985, and 1990 (Thousands)

Household Type	Actual			Projected		
	1960	1970	1975	1980	1985	1990
Married Couple Heads	*39,440*	*43,692*	*47,404*	*47,867*	*49,383*	*50,871*
No Children[a]	17,565	21,384	24,670	23,725	24,209	25,177
One Child	7,449	7,932	9,176	9,372	9,895	10,572
Two or Three Children	11,013	11,187	11,629	12,169	12,851	12,764
Four or More Children	3,413	3,189	1,929	2,601	2,428	2,358
Other Male Head	*4,245*	*6,243*	*7,908*	*10,293*	*12,674*	*14,893*
Single	1,675	2,482	3,441	4,357	5,329	6,336
Previously Married						
No Children	2,314	3,285	4,049	5,357	6,615	7,710
One or More Children	256	476	418	579	730	847
Other Female Head	*9,108*	*13,459*	*17,196*	*20,946*	*24,274*	*26,947*
Single						
No Children	1,445	2,081	2,712	3,477	4,162	4,665
One or More Children	91	286	519	949	1,130	1,186
Divorced/Separated						
No Children	1,397	2,180	3,079	3,885	4,631	5,348
One Child	414	688	1,214	1,456	1,790	2,070
Two or Three Children	489	875	1,404	1,652	1,975	2,084
Four or More Children	198	339	311	520	554	585
Widowed						
No Children	4,517	6,324	7,391	8,414	9,407	10,346
One Child	294	337	282	320	340	370
Two or More Children	263	349	284	273	285	293
TOTAL	52,793	63,394	72,508	79,106	86,331	92,711

SOURCE: John Pitkin and George Masnick, "Analysis and Projection of Housing Consumption by Birth Cohorts: 1960–2000," a research report prepared by the MIT-Harvard Joint Center for Urban Studies for U.S. Department of Housing and Urban Development Grant #H2842RG.
[a] Children under age 15 living at home.

**Table 2.14.   Types of Households in 1960 and 1975 and Projected for 1990
(Percentages)**

	Year		
Household Type	*1960*	*1975*	*1990*
Married Couples	*74.8*	*65.4*	*54.9*
No Children under 15 Present	33.3	34.0	27.2
Children under 15 Present	41.5	31.4	27.7
Other Male Head	*8.1*	*10.9*	*16.0*
Never-Married	3.2	4.7	6.8
Previously Married	4.9	6.2	9.2
No Children under 15 Present	4.4	5.6	8.3
Children under 15 Present	0.5	0.6	0.9
Other Female Head	*17.2*	*23.6*	*29.0*
Never-Married	2.8	4.4	6.3
No Children under 15 Present	2.6	3.7	5.0
Children under 15 Present	0.2	0.7	1.3
Divorced/Separated	4.7	8.2	10.8
No Children under 15 Present	2.6	4.2	5.8
Children under 15 Present	2.1	4.0	5.0
Widowed	9.7	11.0	11.9
No Children under 15 Present	8.6	10.2	11.2
Children under 15 Present	1.1	0.8	0.7

SOURCE: Table 2.13.

slightly more than a quarter of all households. In 1960, 41.5 percent of all households were a married couple with young children.

Male-Headed Households

Before 1970 households headed by unmarried males were relatively rare, both because of the high proportion of adult males who were married and because of the number who lived in institutions, barracks, group quarters, or as boarders or lodgers. In 1960 only 8.1 percent of all households were headed by unmarried males. In recent years, however, the later marriages and higher divorce rates, combined with higher headship rates among the single and divorced, have increased the share of all households headed by unmarried males. By 1990 we project an increase of almost 7 million male-headed households (approximately one-third of all new households), bringing the 1990 share of all households headed by single, widowed, and divorced/separated/spouse-absent males to 16 percent, or twice the 1960 level.

Female-Headed Households

Female-headed households have been in the recent past and will continue to be in the future a major contributor to the increase in total households. Households headed by women increased from 17.2 percent of the total in 1960 to 23.6 percent in 1975. This proportion is projected to increase to 29 percent by 1990, with the addition of almost 10 million female-headed households.

In 1960 widows were the typical female head of household, and over three-quarters of all female-headed households had no children under the age of 15 present. The composition of female-headed households is projected to change as the number of never-married and divorced women increases and as their headship rates continue to rise. The share of female households headed by widows is projected to decline from 56 percent in 1960 to 46 percent in 1975 and to 41 percent in 1990. The share of all households headed by women who have no children under 15 present in the household is not expected to change much between now and 1990, remaining over 75 percent. Even though the growth in female-headed households is going to be weighted in the direction of younger women, who potentially could have young children present, their low fertility is expected to keep the fraction of such households with young children present to below 25 percent of all female-headed households between now and 1990.

Notes

1. Until 1978 the Census Bureau followed a procedure that arbitrarily designated husbands as head of married-couple households. In Figures 2.1 and 2.2 male heads include both husbands and other male heads. Since 1978, data tabulation procedures separate married households headed by married couples from other male- and other female-headed households.

2. For a discussion of the factors associated with the "launching" of children out of the parental household see Cristabel M. Young, "Factors Associated with the Timing and Duration of the Leaving Home Stage of the Family Life Cycle," *Population Studies* 29 (1975), 61–73.

3. Larry Hirschhorn, "Post-Industrial Life: A U.S. Perspective," *Futures* (August 1979), 287–298.

4. John C. Beresford and Alice M. Rivlin, "Privacy, Poverty, and Old Age," *Demography* 3 (1966), 247–258.

5. John C. Beresford and Alice M. Rivlin, "Characteristics of Other Families," *Demography* 1 (1964), 242–246.

6. An influential article on the increase in solo living is that of Frances Kobrin, "The Fall in Household Size and the Rise of the Primary Individual," *Demography* 13 (1976), 127–138.

7. These percentages were calculated from the 1960 Census Public Use Sample and 1975 Annual Housing Survey tapes. Children are those under age 15 who are living at home with their parents.

8. Table 2.3 reports on *net* increases in households which consist of new additions minus dissolutions from each type. New additions to "husband/wife" households include new marriages or departures of already married couples from households headed by some other adult. Dissolutions come from death and divorce. "Other family" households increase through illegitimate childbearing, siblings moving in with each other, and recently divorced individuals moving back to their parents or setting up their own households with their children. The "other family" category loses households when single parents marry or when children move away. "Unrelated individual" households increase when people move to live alone or with non-relatives, when a spouse dies and no children live in the household, or when a relative moves out leaving the household head with no other relatives at home. "Unrelated individual" households decrease in number when couples living together ultimately marry, when people living alone marry, have a child, move in with relatives or die, when a relative moves into an "unrelated individual" household or when the household disbands and all former household members go into non-household quarters (i.e., college dormitories, barracks, prisons, hospitals, etc.) or form families.

9. The year-by-year changes are not reproduced in Table 2.3 but are available in the original source for that table.

10. John Modell and Tamara K. Hareven, "Urbanization and the Malleable Household: An Examination of Boarding and Lodging in American Families," *Journal of Marriage and the Family* (August 1973), 467–479.

11. Paul C. Glick and Arthur J. Norton, "Marrying, Divorcing and Living Together in the U.S. Today," *Population Bulletin* 32 (1977); Frank F. Furstenberg, Jr., "Recycling the Family: Perspectives for a Neglected Family Form," *Marriage and Family Review* 2 (1979), 11–22.

12. *Current Population Reports*, "Demographic Aspects of Aging and the Older Population in the United States," series P-23, no. 59 (May 1976), Table 5-1.

13. Joan Waring, "Social Replenishment and Social Change: The Problem of Disordered Cohort Flaw," *American Behavioral Scientist* 19 (1975), 237–256.

14. We based our projections of headship trends on the pace of change in cohort headship rates over the 1960–1970 period under the hypothesis that the economic and housing conditions of the late 1970s would result in less rapid increases than those of the 1970–1975 period. In addition, we held headship levels for cohorts while under age 30 constant at 1975 levels within the categories of age, sex, marital status and children present. Accordingly, Table 2.12 shows never-married male headship rates constant for those under 30 through 1990. The corresponding female headship rates show a rise over this same period because illegitimate childbearing is projected to shift more never-married women below age 30 into higher headship categories, even though within the categories of age, marital status and presence of children their headship is also held constant at 1975 levels.

Chapter 3

WOMEN'S WORK AND
FAMILY INCOME

A second way in which the households of 1990 will look very different from the households of the late 1970s is in the number of workers they contain. Figure 1.2 shows quite dramatic decreases from 1960 to 1990 in the proportion of one-worker husband/wife households. Over the same period increases are projected for two-worker husband/wife households, one-worker households of single parents and of men and women living alone, and for households with no workers. This chapter explores the dynamics behind those changes, particularly the jump in labor force participation rates of women. Officially the term labor force participation means being at work or looking for work.

The trends suggested by Figure 1.2, however, may be only the tip of the iceberg. Along with shifts in labor force participation, the next decade may see substantial changes in the degree of attachment women have to labor force careers and in their contributions to family income. These latter changes—which, it is important to note, have not yet occurred—are likely to influence in major ways the allocation of time, money and energy within households. They are also likely to create households that are more diverse in both the amount of time and money that is available and in how each is spent. The diversity will, in turn, have important implications for the sorts of choices households make in terms of location, housing, and consumer goods and in demands for public and private services.

Three aspects of women's paid work outside the home should be distinguished from one another: participation, attachment to careers, and contributions to family income. Participants in the labor force are a diverse group. They range from women who spend trifling amounts of time and energy at work to those pursuing full-time careers.

Simple "participation" in the workforce may mean that only the most minor adjustments need be made in women's time use, roles, and perceptions.

"Attachment" is measured by the extent to which a woman's involvement in her work is substantial and permanent. High attachment is characterized by continuous participation over a period of years and by full-time work throughout the year. Women who are strongly attached to careers differ both from women who do not work outside the home and from women whose work attachments are weak. They spend their time differently, and their families function in different ways.

The third aspect of women's work has to do with earnings and contributions to family income. Women who are not in the paid labor force or who are only weakly attached to it are not very likely to contribute much to family income. Even women who are strongly attached labor force participants, however, may hold low-paying jobs and thus be able to contribute relatively small amounts to family income. Both the level of family income and its source—whether it comes from men's earnings, women's earnings, or other income sources—significantly affect family consumption and time allocation patterns.

Of the three aspects of women's work we are considering (participation, attachment and contribution) only the first has changed in any dramatic fashion across the age groups in our three adult generations. The revolution in labor force participation has not extended to attachment or to contribution. From our reading of the data, we believe that a second revolution is just under way in attachment, particularly among the women of the younger generation born after 1940 who also are revolutionizing family structure. A change in relative contributions to family income may be in the wings, but the data are too sketchy to confidently predict its coming on stage.

Labor Force Participation

The rise since World War II in labor force participation of women, especially of wives and mothers, is visible and well publicized. The official estimates are based on participation during the week before the monthly labor force survey is taken and are only a rough description of work activity. Some "participants" are unemployed or marginally employed; some non-participants may have worked at other times during the year or may want to work at the time of the survey. Nonetheless, it is an estimate, which we can compare over time, of the extent to which people work and earn. According to the official estimate, 78.4 percent of men 16 and over and 51.1 percent of women 16 and over were labor force participants in 1979.[1] In that year women made up 42.2 percent of the total civilian labor force in the United States, an increase from 38.2 percent in 1970 and 29.6 percent in 1950.[2] The shift was brought about by a slight reduction in men's participation and a jump in women's participation.

The population pyramids in Figures 3.1 and 3.2 depict how the changing age structure and participation rates from 1950 to 1978 affect the composition of the labor force and the division of the population between workers and non-workers.[3] The pyramids are shaded to show the proportion of men and women by age group who were employed, unemployed, and not in the labor force. For 1960 and 1970 the pyramids also divide the employed between full-time and part-time workers.

The shifting age structure of the labor force reflects the shifting age structure of the population as a whole which was caused by the older generation's Depression-linked low birthrates and the middle generation's post-war baby boom. In 1960 and 1970 the largest employed groups were in the pyramids' middle age ranges; by 1978 the younger baby boom generation was beginning to move into the labor force, creating a bulge at earlier ages. By 1990, when the younger generation is in its late 20s and 30s, its behavior will have a strong impact on the labor force.

Almost all 25- to 60-year-old men were employed every year from 1950 to 1978.[4] Employment rates of older men have declined, a sign of earlier and partial retirement. Employment rates of men under 25 fluctuate, probably because of short-term economic conditions, changes in the size of the armed forces, and changing rates of school enrollment.

Women have made the biggest changes in the labor force, as shown on the right side of the population pyramids. Since the proportion of women in the labor force has been moving up in all age groups, the 1978 female pyramid resembles the male pyramid much more closely than was the case in 1950. Employment has increased both over the life course of one group and in succeeding age groups. The proportion of 25- to 29-year-old women who are employed, for example, has increased steadily from 1950 to 1978. At the same time, a comparison of women age 25–29 in 1950 with 35- to 39-year-olds in 1960, 45- to

49-year-olds in 1970, and 55- to 59-year-olds in 1978 shows that women born between 1921 and 1925 kept adding their numbers to the labor force over that time.

In addition to illustrating information about workers, the population pyramids also point out changes in the number and character of non-workers. In 1950, prime-age women, 25–60, made up a substantial portion of the nonworking population. In 1960 and 1970 children dominated the nonworking population (young children in 1960 and teenagers in 1970). By 1978 older men and women were beginning to be an important component of the nonworking population. As the population ages over the next decade, men and women over 60 will become an increasingly larger proportion of total nonworkers. This increase, however, will be offset by the entry of the baby boom into the workforce. Workers as a percentage of the total population will thus continue to increase much as they have in the past. Workers moved from 37.8 percent of the population in 1960 to 47.1 percent in 1978.

Predicting the shape the population pyramids will take in 1980 and 1990 requires attention to labor force participation rates by age groupings, our next topic.

Age Patterns (Period Data)

Both men's and women's participation in the labor force varies with age. Smaller proportions of young men work than do men age 25–54; the latter's participation rate in 1978 was 92.7 percent. Male participation falls gradually after age 55 and more steeply after age 65. In 1978 men 65 and over had a participation rate of 19.6 percent. The age and participation patterns of women are much more complicated.

Figure 3.3 plots labor force participation rates by each year of age from 20 to 70 for 1940, 1950, 1960, and 1970 for women, and for 1970 for men. These more detailed age data still show the pattern for men to be quite simple. Participation rises gradually to the mid-20s, and then levels off until the mid-50s. (The pattern has hardly changed over time. Since the curves for 1950 and 1960 for men were almost identical to those for 1970, we did not enter them into Figure 3.3.)

Women's participation rates after 1940, in contrast, show an "M" pattern: rising from the late teens until the early 20s, falling until the late 20s (their childbearing and child-rearing years), rising again until the middle and late 40s and falling during the 50s and after.

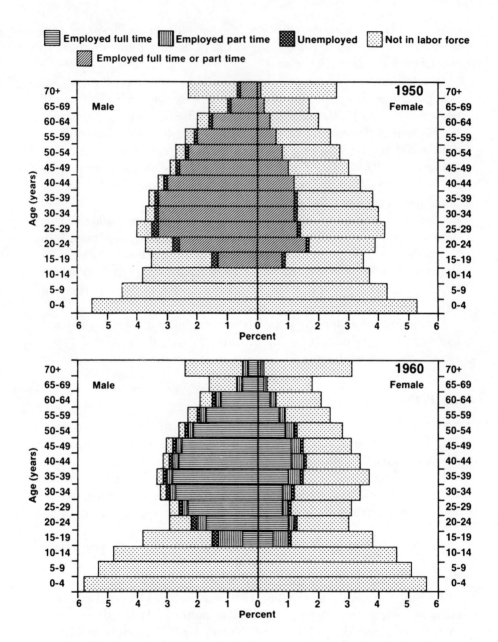

Figure 3.1. Population by Labor Force Status, 1950 and 1960. *(Source: Appendix Tables C.1. a and b.)*

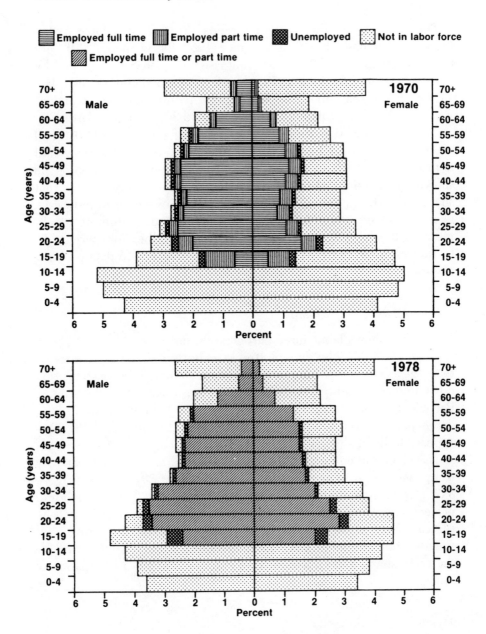

Figure 3.2. Population by Labor Force Status, 1970 and 1978. *(Source: Appendix Tables C.1. c and d.)*

   The age curves show, as the pyramids did, that labor force participation rates have been rising since 1950 for women at all ages
between 20 and 55. (The continuing rise since 1970 is suggested by
the dashed line showing 1979 labor force participation rates.) The
curves also suggest that the participation pattern may be changing,
with the "M" dip for women in their 20s and 30s gradually flattening. ·

   One might predict, then, that the curves for women in 1980 and
1990 would not only be the same shape as those for men but would
approach the levels of men as well. The broken line in Figure 3.3
showing projections of the 1990 female labor force does assume that
shape. The disappearing "M" curve could be expected to indicate a
new life-course pattern for women, one of high and continuing attachment to the labor force even through the childbearing period. To
further examine both of these issues, we must turn to data on birth
cohorts.

Age Patterns (Cohort Data)

Figure 3.4 shows labor force participation for cohorts born 1901–05
through 1951–55. The data plotted by cohort are even more striking
than the earlier data for particular years. Labor force participation
rates increase steadily from older to younger in almost all age groups.
Participation of age cohorts born before 1940 show a distinct "M"
curve pattern, but among younger cohorts the trough of the "M"
appears to be shallower and to occur at an earlier age.

   The changing cohort patterns can be shown even more clearly by
using single year of age data for women in their 20s and 30s (Figure
3.5). These curves show the "M" dip for cohorts before 1945 and
project its gradual flattening out among women born after 1945. The
regular shape of the curves gives some hints about the future, and
suggests that the labor force participation of women in 1990 will be
the same shape and approach the same levels as the participation of
men.

Marital Status Patterns

The patterns and projections presented thus far have been based only
on age data. One way to check on the logic of the projections is to
compare the conclusions with data on labor force participation by
marital and family status.

   Traditionally, women's decisions to work or not have been tied to

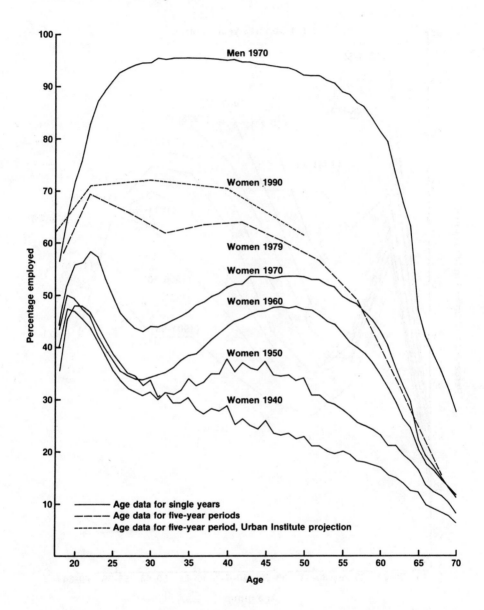

Figure 3.3.   Labor Force Participation Rates for Men and Women by Age, 1940–1990. *(Source: Appendix Tables C. 3. a and b.)*

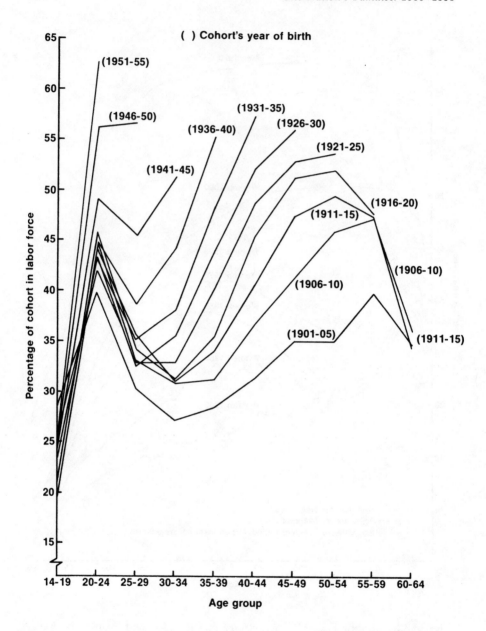

Figure 3.4.   Labor Force Participation Rates for Birth Cohorts of American Women. *(Source: Appendix Table C. 4.)*

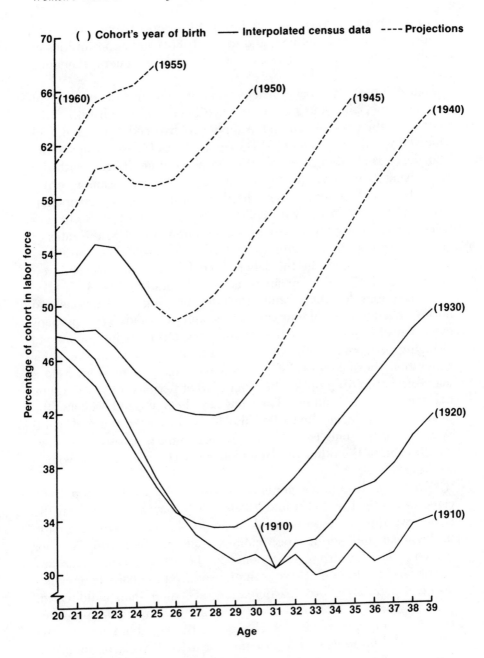

Figure 3.5. Labor Force Participation Rates for Selected Birth Cohorts of American Women Age 20–39. *(Source: Appendix Tables C. 5. a and b.)*

decisions about marriage and children, to norms of appropriate behavior for wives and mothers, and to constraints and opportunities in
the fluctuating demand for women workers and in general economic
conditions.

Figure 3.6 shows that participation rates among never-married
women, especially young women, have been quite high from 1950
right up to the present. The same applies to divorced, separated, and
widowed women below age 60. The percentage of these groups in the
labor force is climbing toward 80 to 85 percent at all ages, with the
rates rising even more quickly at older ages. Married women, especially those with children, show the sharpest increase in participation
rates. Within the group with children, the greatest increase in participation is among those with young children. In 1978, the rates of
married women living with their husbands reached an unprecedented 37.6 percent in the labor force for women with children
under 3, and 47.9 percent for women with children age 3–5.

Explanations for these shifts include changing expectations and
norms, changing economic pressures and demands, or—perhaps
most plausibly—a combination of adjusting attitudes in response to
changing economic conditions. For example, women in the older
generation (born before 1920) may have expected to work before
marriage but to drop out of the labor market permanently when they
became wives and mothers. They may have been pushed back into the
paid work force during the 1930s and 1940s by the Depression and World
War II, in the one case by severe economic pressures on their
families and in the other by strong labor market demands for women
workers.[5]

Women of the middle generation (born between 1920 and 1940)
came of age in the 1940s and 1950s. They may have felt both the
strong wartime and post-war demand for labor, especially in the
professional and service occupations traditionally appropriate for
women, and the strong sentiments in the 1950s for marriage and
childbearing. Although these women produced the baby boom, they
also had high labor force participation rates after their childbearing
years. Their high rates may have been induced by work opportunities, by economic needs, by changed attitudes about the relative
satisfactions to be gained from family or market work, or simply by
inertia.

Women of the younger generation (born after 1940) are marrying
later and having fewer children at a later time in life. Before marriage
their labor force participation rates are high. By working in their 20s,

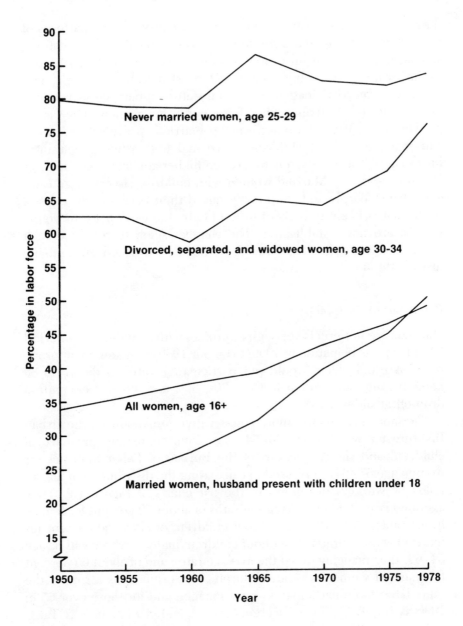

Figure 3.6. Labor Force Participation Rates for Selected Groups of Women, 1950–1978. (*Source: Appendix Tables C . 6 . a and b .)*

they may establish positive expectations about work and patterns of work generally, which are reinforced by the difficulty of maintaining standards of living in unsettled economic times. Changing attitudes toward women's roles both shape and are shaped by work behavior.

The data on participation by marital status support our projections of a rising and flattening labor force curve for women. The fastest growing categories of women—never-married, previously married, and married without children—have had high participation rates historically. These are likely to go even higher among women in their 30s, 40s, and 50s. Married women with children, a very large category, have sharply and continually raised their participation rates, a trend that is likely to be kept in motion by the work patterns young women are now establishing. The changes seem to reinforce each other, and it is difficult to foresee a dynamic that would substantially disrupt them.

Participation in 1990

Our data are not precise enough to project with confidence numerical labor force participation in 1990; even our 1980 estimates are approximate. A rough guess would put participation rates in the 70 to 80 percent range for women in their 20s, 30s, and 40s in 1990 (with a drop-off at older ages).

The more precise and more conservative projections of the Urban Institute for women age 20–54 by marital status and presence of children, and the projections of the Bureau of Labor Statistics for women age 55–64, were used in calculating the distribution of households by workers presented in the bar charts of Figure 1.2. They assumed labor force participation rates of about 70 percent for female heads under 65, with and without children; of about 60 percent for married women under 65 without children (many of whom will be age 54–65, thus bringing down the average rate); and of about 65 percent for married women without children. The projections assumed the same labor force participation rates for men and for those over 65 in 1990 as in 1978. (The projections are explained in Appendix Table B.1.)

Another approach to estimates of the future is to look at the labor force participation of unmarried women in their 20s and 30s. In 1978, 86.6 percent of never-married women age 25–34 participated in the labor force, while divorced women age 25–34 with no children had a 91.1 percent rate. This suggests a much higher upper boundary for women's participation than the rates we projected for 1990. Interestingly, black and other minority men of the same age (25–34) have participation rates around 85 percent. The similar rates for both women and minority men may have something to do with labor markets and the country's unemployment rates.

It is probably also the case, however, that most women who have children will continue to stop working or to cut back for some period of time. How these interruptions will affect labor force participation rates depends not only on what women actually do (how long and how often they stop working) but also on how they report their status to the labor force survey during that period. It is entirely possible for mothers to leave their jobs for six months or a year around each birth, but to think of themselves and to report themselves as temporarily out of work or unemployed and thus to be counted in the labor force. If they work at all, no matter how few hours a week, they are reported not only as in the labor force but also as employed. Considerable attention to the duties of motherhood, therefore, can be consistent with very high rates of labor force participation.

It is our hunch that today's very high labor force participation rates in the younger generation reflect these attitudes. Almost all young women work at some point; most may look on work as the normal course of events and on periods of non-work as temporary. It is entirely possible that married women with children will think of themselves as being in the labor force almost continuously and that their *reported* participation rates will approach those of unmarried women and minority men.

Being "in the labor force," of course, does not necessarily mean working either full time or continuously. High labor force participation rates among women in their 20s and 30s can mask wide fluctuations in work schedules to accommodate child care. The reported rates now mask much of the movement back and forth between paid work and child care; they may do so even more in the future. As women's labor force participation rates approach or even exceed 80 to 85 percent, which we believe they will, it becomes increasingly important to know just what that means.

Labor Force Attachment

Women's work will be more important to women themselves, to families, and to the society generally if it is substantial and permanent rather than temporary and part-time. The official category of "labor force participants," which includes the entire range of hours and years worked, should be refined so that we can understand the extent to which changes are actually taking place. We can narrow the definition somewhat by looking at two characteristics of labor force attachment: (1) full-time full-year work and (2) number of years in the labor force.

Type of Work Experience

The labor force population pyramids in Figures 3.1 and 3.2 divide the employed in 1960 and 1970 into full-time (35 hours or more per week) and part-time workers. In 1960 and 1970 about two-thirds of the women workers were full time, a proportion that changes very little over time. Part-time work was most common among very young workers but not unusual among any of the groups.

Part-time work, however, is only one indication of the extent of labor force attachment. Equally important is whether women work all year or on an intermittent or seasonal basis. We turn, therefore, to an analysis of full-time full-year work by women.

Figure 3.7, which includes data for men and women by age groups, plots labor force participation rates in March 1978, proportions who worked at all during 1977, and proportions working full time for 50 to 52 weeks during 1977. The proportions who had worked any time during the year are consistently higher than the labor force participation rates. That is because more people work at some point during the course of a year than are working at the one point when the official surveys are made. For both men and women, though, work during the year and labor force participation rates match pretty closely— especially after age 24—and show similar age patterns. The distance between the two curves is somewhat wider for women than for men, which suggests that women move in and out of the labor force more often than men.

The proportions of age groups who work full time for 50 to 52 weeks during the year are well below the work-at-all curves, especially for women. Among males age 25–54, about three-quarters of those who had worked during the year were year-round full-time workers; among women age 25–54 less than half of those who had worked were year-round full-time. Only about a third of all women age 25–54, in fact, were year-round full-time workers in 1977.

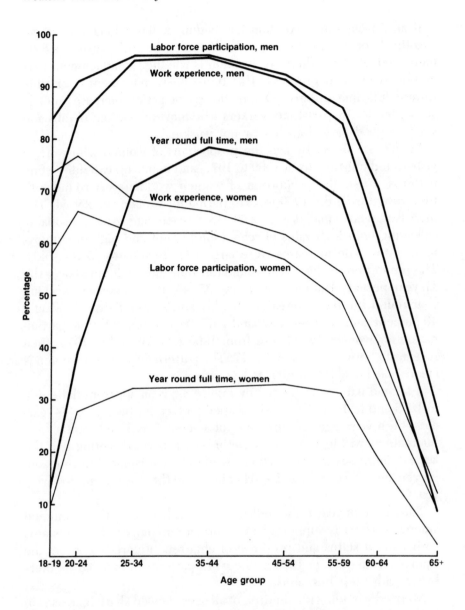

Figure 3.7. Labor Force Participation in 1978 and Percentage Working Year-Round Full-Time in 1977. *(Source: Appendix Table C. 7.)*

If an attachment revolution has begun, it has a long way to go: two-thirds of the 25- to 54-year-old women in 1977 were not fully employed. Perhaps the next question is whether an attachment revolution is even in progress. Has there been movement over time toward full-time careers? Or are the participation increases mostly accounted for by part-time workers who move in and out of jobs and spend a good part of each year not working?

Figure 3.8 shows by age the proportions of women who worked year-round full-time from 1960 to 1977, and points up two interesting patterns. First, the proportion of women working year-round full-time rose during the 1960 to 1970 period for women age 25–54. The increases were small for the 20- to 24-year age group, probably reflecting both high rates of school enrollment and high unemployment rates. The increases were largest for the 24- to 35-year-olds. The proportion working year-round full-time almost doubled over the 17-year period. Among women age 35–44, the proportion working year-round full-time increased steadily and substantially, showing a 40 percent gain between 1960 and 1977. Year-round full-time participation for women 45–59 rose from 1960 to 1970, fell in 1975, then rose again between 1975 and 1977. The pattern for younger women is clear; that for older women is less so.

A second pattern suggested by Figure 3.8 is an apparent flattening in 1975 and in 1977 of the "M"-shaped pattern for the 24- to 35-year-olds. Ten-year age groups can, of course, mask substantial age fluctuations within a group. Nonetheless, it is worth noting that the largest increases in proportions working year-round full-time occurred among women age 25–34, who are in their prime child-rearing years.

The idea that year-round full-time work is becoming more common among mothers is supported by information comparing work status with marital status and presence of children. Figure 3.9 shows the changes from 1960 to 1978 in the work patterns of married mothers living with their husbands.

Married women with children of all ages showed sharp increases in both full- and part-time work from 1960 to 1978. Among women with school-age children, year-round full-time work increased more steeply than part-time work and accounted for most of the increase in the proportions who worked at all. By 1978 the proportion working year-round full-time exceeded the proportion working part-time. Among those mothers of school-age children with work experience, about 40 percent were working year-round full-time.

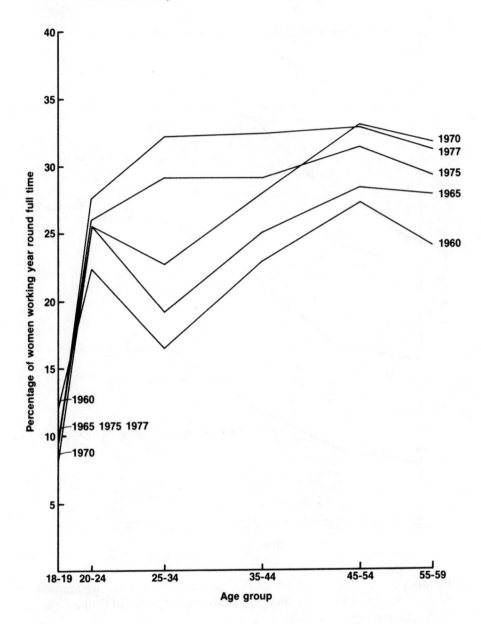

Figure 3.8.   Percentage of Women Working Year-Round Full-Time by Age, 1960–1977. (*Source: Appendix Table C. 8.*)

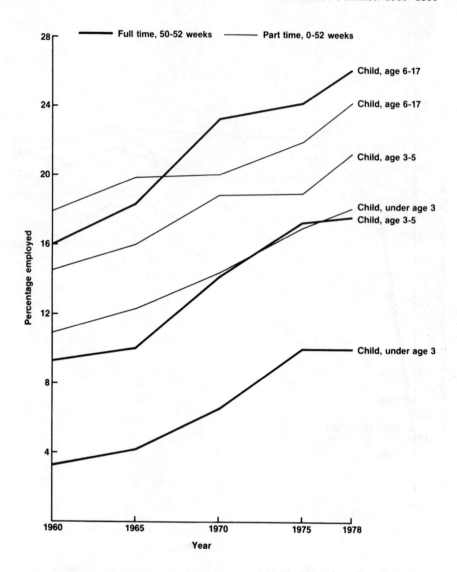

Figure 3.9.   Percentage Working Year-Round Full-Time among Married Women, Husband Present with Children, by Age of Youngest Child, 1960–1978. *(Source: Appendix Table C . 9.)*

Among women with children age 3–5, year-round full-time work increased more sharply than part-time work. In 1978 about a third of this group who had work experience were year-round full-time workers. About half of the increase in work experience between 1960 and 1977 in this group was accounted for by an increase in year-round full-time work and about half by part-time work.

Among mothers of children under 3, about a fifth of those with work experience (roughly 10 percent of all mothers with children under 3) were year-round full-time workers. For that group, the sharp increases in part-time work were what caused most of the increase between 1960 and 1978 in the proportion with work experience.

Taken together, the data point to a picture of gradually increasing attachment to the labor force among women. Full-time year-round workers are increasing as a proportion of all groups whether based on age, marital status, or ages of children. But by no means is all of the recent sharp increase in labor force participation accounted for by fully employed women, even among the young. For women with young children, much of the movement into the labor force has been into part-time and part-year work. Though fewer mothers are dropping out of the labor force, they continue to adjust their work lives to the demands of home and children.

Continuity of Labor Force Experience

Table 3.1 shows the number of years women age 18–47 worked from 1968 to 1977. It is divided between women who were wives all ten years and women who headed families without husbands all ten years. Working was defined as earning more than $100 in a year.

The table shows a fair amount of movement between working and non-working status for both wives and unmarried heads. Eighty-two percent of the wives had earnings at least one year out of the ten. Only about 21 percent of the wives, however, had earnings all ten years. Another 62 percent worked between one and nine years. If we define working at least seven years out of ten as a measure of relatively permanent attachment to work, slightly less than half (44 percent) of the women who had been married all ten years fell into the permanent category.

Women without husbands who headed households all ten years had more permanent work histories. (Remaining a head for ten years is a relatively unusual occurrence. Most divorced women remarry less

Table 3.1. **Proportion of Women with Earnings for Specific Lengths of Time, 1968–1977**

Age in 1968		Number of Years with Earnings				
	n	0	1–3	4–6	7–9	10
Wives						
18–27	352	13.6	22.4	23.5	24.4	15.9
28–37	472	15.7	23.1	16.6	25.2	19.5
38–47	464	22.8	18.7	12.9	20.5	25.0
Total	1,288	17.7	21.4	17.2	23.4	20.5
Heads						
18–27	48	14.6	10.5	8.4	14.6	52.1
28–37	126	13.5	19.8	12.0	13.5	41.3
38–47	167	12.0	13.8	9.0	19.2	46.1
Total	341	12.9	15.6	9.9	16.4	45.2

SOURCE: Tabulations from the Panel Study of Income Dynamics, 1968–1977 by Neal Baer. Percentages do not always add to 100 because of rounding error.

than five years after the divorce.) Eighty-seven percent of these women had earnings in at least one of the ten years, and 45 percent had earnings all ten years. Among this group of women, nearly two-thirds (62 percent) qualify as permanent workers according to our seven-out-of-ten-year criterion.

Patterns of labor force attachment vary by age as well as by marital status. When we compared, for example, married women age 18–27 in 1968 (born 1941–1950) with those who were 10 and 20 years older, we found that attachment to the labor force (seven out of ten years) increased with age (Table 3.1). Of the married women age 38–47 in 1968 (born 1921–1930), 46 percent worked at least seven out of the ten years between 1968 and 1977. The attachment of those born between 1931 and 1940 was slightly less (45 percent), while the youngest age group's rate of 40 percent was lowest of all. Interestingly, this trend is reversed if we look at the proportions having zero compared with one or more years of work experience. Only 14 percent of the younger group had no earnings over the ten years, whereas 23 percent of the older group did not work at all. Young women in the sample were more likely to be workers at some point, but older women were more likely, if they worked, to have worked continuously.

One explanation for this pattern of stronger attachment with increasing age pertains to stage of the life course. The oldest age grouping, which was between the ages 38–47 in 1968 and 47–56 in 1977, had finished both bearing and rearing young children. Younger women, on the other hand, may have been less strongly attached to the labor force because they were in school or they took time off to start and raise families.

We also compared women 18–27, 28–37, and 38–47 years old who were unmarried heads over the ten-year period. Not surprisingly, Table 3.1 shows that single women's permanent attachment to the labor force is stronger than that of married women. Both the youngest and oldest age groupings had a permanent attachment rate close to two-thirds. That of the middle group (born 1931–1940), however, was only 55 percent.

Attachment in 1990

The labor force participation of women during the 1970s was both more widespread and less permanent than is generally realized. Over a period of several years, a large majority of women worked, but only a minority worked full-time all year. An even smaller minority worked full-time all year for several years. Most women were in and out of the labor force; many worked part-time. In most cases, women adjusted their work schedules to accommodate family responsibilities. Few demanded substantial changes in family organization to accommodate their work schedules.

Changes in the latter direction may, however, be down the road. Year-round full-time workers are becoming a larger proportion of both age groups and of workers. This is especially true among young women.[6] Attachment, however, is surely not keeping pace with the participation revolution. The picture is much too unclear even to predict with accuracy the proportions of women who will take on continuous full-time work careers, or the extent they will work throughout the time they have young children.

Contributions to Family Income

In assessing the scope and implications of the "revolution" in women's work, we cannot ignore their contributions to family income. The issues, of course, vary from one household to another. In traditional husband/wife families, the wife's contributions may do little more than alter saving and spending decisions.

In female-headed families, women's work and earnings can make the difference between poverty and an adequate living standard, and between independence or a dependence on alimony, help from relatives, or public welfare. Female-headed families are able to make it on their own only when the woman has regular work and adequate earnings.

For unmarried women without children, the issue is apt to be whether their earnings are enough to support an independent household. With adequate incomes, young women can live independently of their parents and older women can live independently of their children.

Potentially, changes in women's work and earnings could transform the income and life-style patterns among different types of households: between one- and two-worker husband/wife households; between male and female family heads; between men and women living alone; and between husband/wife and other types of households. When added to changes in the distribution of types of households, these work and earnings changes could create a fundamentally different landscape of households—that is, different spending patterns, demands for time- or money-saving goods and services and demands for public services.

Households, Work, and Income

Labor force attachment, not mere participation, is the real issue behind potential changes in household income. Figure 3.10 depicts working and non-working households in 1977, based on whether or not the head worked year-round full-time. Mean income is also shown for the different types of households. A few of the facts shown by Figure 3.10 are particularly relevant:

1. The difference between labor force participation and working year-round full-time (seen by comparing Figure 3.10 with the 1975 bar in Figure 1.2):

   —The proportion of no-worker husband/wife households is twice as large if working is defined as year-round full-time.

   —The proportion of female heads working drops from about a half to a third when working is defined as year-round full-time.

   —If working wives were defined as year-round full-time, the proportion of two-worker households would fall to about 10

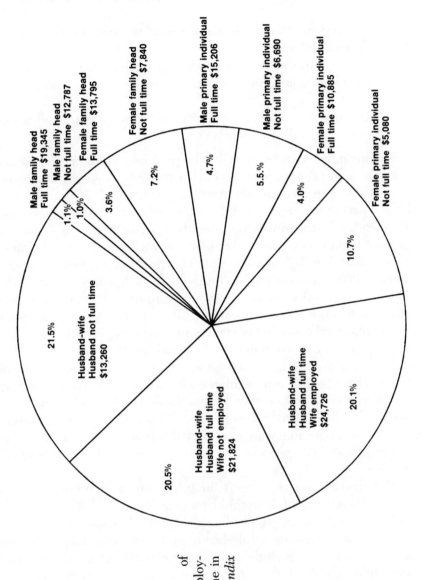

Male family head
Full time $19,345

Male family head
Not full time $12,787

Female family head
Full time $13,795

Female family head
Not full time $7,840

Male primary individual
Full time $15,206

Male primary individual
Not full time $6,690

Female primary individual
Full time $10,885

Female primary individual
Not full time $5,080

Husband-wife
Husband not full time
$13,260

Husband-wife
Husband full time
Wife not employed
$21,824

Husband-wife
Husband full time
Wife employed
$24,726

1.1%
1.0%
3.6%
7.2%
4.7%
5.5.%
4.0%
10.7%
21.5%
20.5%
20.1%

Figure 3.10. Types of Households and Employ-ment with Mean Income in 1977. *(Source: Appendix Table C. 10.)*

percent, since only about half of working wives work full-time all year.

2. The smallness of the average income differential between one- and two-worker husband/wife families—that is, only about $3000.

3. The substantial income differentials between male and female year-round full-time workers.

The mean incomes by household type shown in Figure 3.10 reflect both the effects of working and other differences among the household types. The income differences are substantial, as can be shown by comparing the mean incomes of the different types of households. Two-worker husband/wife households had incomes in 1977 about 13 percent higher than one-worker husband/wife households. The difference of $3000 in 1977 was accounted for by wives' average earnings of about $6000 which were offset by about $3000 less income from other sources—most often in the husbands' earnings.[7] No household type other than two-worker households had an average income as high as that of one-worker husband/wife families. Average income was higher in households that contained year-round full-time workers, and income was higher for men than for women. The income of male family heads who were full-time workers, for example, averaged 89 percent of the income of one-worker husband/wife families, while male primary individuals averaged 70 percent. At the other extreme, women who lived alone and who were not full-time workers had average incomes only 23 percent of those of one-worker husband/wife families.

The distribution represents an interesting and perhaps unprecedented diversity of household income levels and life-style possibilities. High-income households include husband-wife families, full-time working male family heads, and men living alone. Medium-income households include many of those in the category of husband/wife families without a full-time working husband (retired couples, for example) and full-time working female family heads and women living alone. Low-income households include female family heads and men and women living alone who are not working full-time.

This diversity in households will increase as we move toward 1990. We project increasing labor force participation by women and, more slowly, their increasing attachment to the labor force. Projections call for growth in two-worker compared with one-worker husband/wife families, in working compared with non-working single-parent families, and in the households of working women (under 65) living alone.

This household diversity has, we think, interesting implications for a variety of economic and social issues. Before moving to those issues it is useful, however, to ask further questions about household diversity: What are the trends in average income differentials among different types of households? That is to say, are two-worker and one-worker households likely to remain so close in average income? Are male- and female-headed households likely to have more equal incomes? Are non-working, partly working, and fully working households likely to maintain their current income differentials?

Table 3.2 shows the changes between 1960 and 1975 in the average income of various household types compared with the mean income of married couples with children. In general, the income of the other types stayed about the same relative to that of married couples with children. Only two changes are noteworthy, one for female heads with children and the other for single or previously married women over 65 (mostly widows). Both groups improved their income position relative to married couples with children between 1960 and 1975. The improvements for female-headed families could be due to increases either in hours worked (which we have already suggested took place), in wages, or in public assistance. Improvements for women over 65 are most likely to have come from transfer payments.

Table 3.2.   Ratio of Income of Different Household Types to Income of Married Couples with Children, 1960–1975

	Ratio		
Household Type	*1960*	*1970*	*1975*
Married Couples with Children	100	100	100
Married Couples, No Children			
Wife under Age 35	97	91	94
Wife 35–64	102	102	103
Wife 65+	56	55	56
Men Single or Previously Married, No Children			
Man under Age 65	65	62	65
Man 65+	35	32	37
Men with Children	68	69	71
Women with Children	30	34	40
Women Single or Previously Married, No Children			
Woman under Age 65	43	41	45
Woman 65+	22	23	29

SOURCE: Tabulations of 1960 and 1970 Census Public Use Samples and 1975 Annual Housing Survey tapes by John Pitkin.

Two-Worker Families

In 1977 working wives brought in on average about a quarter of family income. Table 3.3 shows the percentage contribution of employed wives from 1960 to 1977. Surprisingly, the portion of family income that wives contribute in two-worker families has hardly changed, either overall or within full-time and part-time work categories. The consistently low percentages from 1960 to 1977 will not necessarily continue into the future. It is worth asking, to start, if young women are establishing a different pattern.

In young families (wives age 14–24), 71 percent of the wives had earnings in 1976 and contributed 30 percent of the earnings of two-earner families. In families where the wives were aged 25–44, 61 percent of wives had earnings and contributed 28 percent of the earnings of two-earner families. As with participation and attachment, the earnings pattern for younger women differs somewhat from that of older women.

Table 3.4 shows the percentage of married women earning 20 percent and 33 percent of family income over a ten-year period. Only seven percent of the wives contributed more than 20 percent of total income in all ten years; only 2.1 percent contributed 33 percent or more in every year of the ten-year period. At the opposite extreme, in 45 percent of the families wives never once contributed more than 20 percent; in two-thirds of the families wives never once contributed at least 33 percent. These last two figures are slightly misleading because they include both families with wives who worked and those who never entered the labor force over the ten-year period. If we look only at wives who worked, we find that one-third of all the

Table 3.3. Contributions to Family Income of Employed Wives, 1960–1977

	Median Percentage of Family Income			
Time with Earnings	1960	1965	1970	1977
Full Time, 50–52 Weeks	38.1	38.1	37.8	38.2
Full Time, 27–49 Weeks	31.6	30.4	29.8	29.8
Part Time or Less than 27 Weeks	(5.7)	(6.9)	11.7	11.1
Total	(20.0)	(22.1)	26.5	26.1

SOURCES: Department of Labor, *Special Labor Force Reports*, "Marital and Family Characteristics of Workers, 1970–78," nos. 13, 64, 130 and 219.

NOTE: Percentages in parentheses include wives with unpaid work experience; not comparable with 1970 and later.

Table 3.4. **Proportion of Women Earning Greater than 20 and 33 Percent of Family Income for Specific Lengths of Time, 1968–1977**

	Years with Earnings Greater than 20 Percent				
Age in 1968	*0*	*1–3*	*4–6*	*7–9*	*10*
18–27	35.2	28.4	15.3	16.2	4.8
28–37	45.8	20.2	14.2	12.0	7.8
38–47	51.7	15.5	9.5	15.5	7.8
Total	45.0	20.7	12.8	14.4	7.0
	Years with Earnings Greater than 33 Percent				
18–27	51.7	27.3	11.3	8.9	0.9
28–37	64.0	19.0	7.9	6.2	3.0
38–47	69.0	16.5	7.1	5.1	2.2
Total	62.4	20.4	8.6	6.5	2.1

SOURCE: See Appendix Table C.11. Percentages do not always add to 100 due to rounding error.

working wives never earned more than 20 percent of the family income in any given year.

The more years a wife had worked, the more likely she was to have had earnings greater than 20 percent of the total family income. Of those wives who worked two out of the ten years, only 9.5 percent earned more than 20 percent of family income for both years. Among those wives who worked all ten years, over a third had earnings greater than 20 percent of the total family income every year. Married women with a strong attachment to the labor force, whether they choose to work or have to for financial reasons, undoubtedly get better paying jobs than those who move in and out of the workforce.

A smaller portion of young women (35 percent) never had any yearly earnings greater than 20 percent, compared with 46 percent of those born between 1931 and 1940 and 52 percent of those born between 1921 and 1930. A larger percentage of the older group had earnings for all ten years that were greater than 20 percent of the total family income—7.8 percent compared with 4.8 percent of the 18- to 27-year-olds.

These data suggest that wives' contributions to family income are likely to increase as their labor force attachment increases. They also suggest that, on the average, wives' contributions over a period of years are rather small. Their contributions do, however, make a substantial difference in the income levels of their families. Table 3.5 defines six income levels, from poor to rich based on income from all

Table 3.5.   Wives' Contribution to Family Income Level, 1971

Living Level	No children	Children
Based on All but Wife's Income		
Percentage of Couples without Working Wives		
Poor[a]	9.1	13.2
Near Poor[b]	6.4	16.3
Getting Along[c]	18.6	30.7
Comfortable[d]	24.3	15.6
Prosperous[e]	31.2	15.6
Rich[f]	10.5	5.1
Percentage of Couples with Working Wives		
Poor	9.5	16.4
Near Poor	11.9	21.0
Getting Along	23.3	29.1
Comfortable	21.1	20.8
Prosperous	27.2	9.9
Rich	7.1	2.8
Based on Total Family Income		
Percentage of Couples with Working Wives		
Poor	1.2	5.9
Near Poor	1.3	12.0
Getting Along	9.8	24.4
Comfortable	17.8	26.7
Prosperous	45.1	25.6
Rich	22.8	5.4

SOURCE: Tabulations by Lee Rainwater from the Panel Study of Income Dynamics 1971 panel, as reported in "Mothers' Contribution to the Family Money Economy in Europe and America," *Joint Center Family Policy Note* 12 (1979).

[a] Less than half of median income.
[b] 50–70 percent of median income.
[c] 70–100 percent of median income.
[d] 100–130 percent of median income.
[e] 130–200 percent of median income.
[f] More than twice median income.

sources except wives' income and shows the percentage of both working wife and non-working wife couples at each level. Without wives' earnings, about 9.5 percent of working-wife families without children and about 16.4 percent of families with children would have been poor; about 44.7 percent of working-wife families without children and 66.5 percent of families with children would have been below the comfortable level. Non-working-wife families were somewhat better off, which suggests that wives tend to work when family income is lower.

Table 3.5 also shows the distribution of working-wife families by income level with wives' income included. Among working-wife couples with no children, the proportion defined as poor has fallen from 9.5 to 1.2 percent, implying that 88 percent of families were moved out of poverty by wives' earnings. Among couples with children, 52 percent were moved out of poverty by wives' earnings. The proportion of working-wife couples with no children at the comfortable or above levels increased from 55.4 percent to 85.7 percent, while 72 percent moved from getting along or below to comfortable or above. Among families with children, 36 percent of those at the poor, near poor, or getting along levels were moved to comfortable or above by wives' earnings.

In short, wives' earnings often move their families out of poverty and, more generally, to higher living levels. This effect is likely to become even more important over the next decade as wives' attachment to the labor force increases.

Single-Parent Families

The income of women who head families, mostly single parents living with children, is much lower than that of two-parent households (see Figure 3.10). These differences in average income between one- and two-parent families occur partly because low-income families are more likely to divorce, separate, or have one of the spouses die than are higher income families. Most of the difference, however, occurs because family income must be shared between two households and is not always shared equitably. Figures 3.11 and 3.12 (and Appendix Table C.12) show mean incomes of divorced, separated, and widowed women with children. All experience a decline in family income between the last year of marriage and the first year after the break, which is by and large not recovered during the following three years. Widowed women experience less sharp income declines than the divorced and separated, though their beginning income position is lower. Women in the upper-income levels have larger income declines than others, but they begin and also end up at higher levels.

Earnings of single mothers are the most important source of income for their households, providing on the average between 60 and 70 percent of family income. As we would expect, women who are unmarried and household heads contribute more to their family income than married women contribute to theirs. Table 3.6 presents the data for 1968 to 1977 on years unmarried women had earnings.

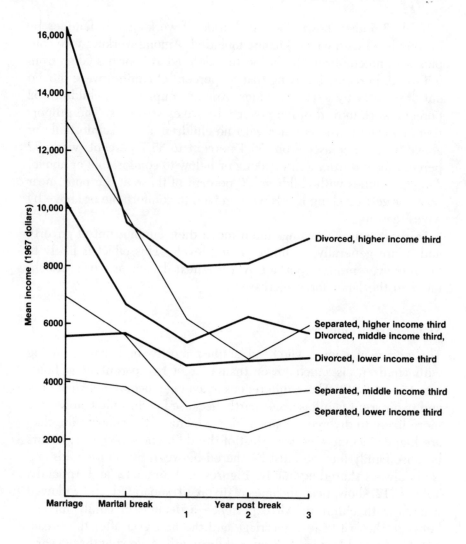

Figure 3.11.   Mean Family Income of Mothers before and after Divorce or Separation by Income Thirds during Marriage, 1968–1977. *(Source: Appendix Table C. 12.)*

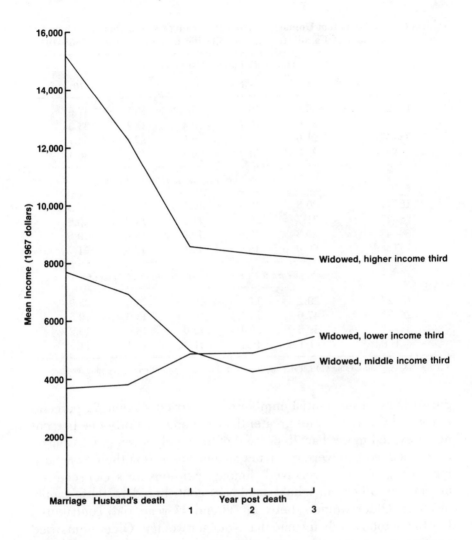

Figure 3.12. Mean Family Income of Widowed Mothers before and after Death of Husband by Income Thirds during Marriage, 1968–1977. *(Source: Appendix Table C.12.)*

**Table 3.6.   Proportion of Unmarried Women Earning Greater than 20, 50, and 75
Percent of Family Income for Specific Lengths of Time, 1968–1977**

Age in 1968	Years with Earnings Greater than 20 Percent				
	0	1–3	4–6	7–9	10
18–27	18.8	10.5	6.3	16.8	47.9
28–37	24.6	16.7	10.4	15.1	33.3
38–47	21.6	11.4	9.6	22.8	34.7
Total	22.3	13.2	9.3	19.1	36.1
	Years with Earnings Greater than 50 Percent				
18–27	20.8	10.4	10.5	27.2	31.3
28–37	31.7	22.3	11.2	14.3	20.6
38–47	29.3	18.0	13.2	19.8	19.8
Total	29.0	18.5	12.0	18.8	21.7
	Years with Earnings Greater than 75 Percent				
18–27	29.2	14.7	10.5	23.0	22.9
28–37	47.6	19.1	10.4	13.6	9.5
38–47	39.5	20.4	12.0	18.0	10.2
Total	41.1	19.1	11.1	17.1	11.7

SOURCE: See Appendix Table C.13. Percentages do not always add to 100 due to rounding error.

Surprisingly, a substantial number of unmarried women (22 percent)
never had yearly incomes greater than 20 percent. Forty-one percent
never earned more than 75 percent of the yearly income. Obviously,
unmarried women were receiving income apart from their own earnings. They may have received alimony, pensions, or social security,
or perhaps other household members contributed to these family
incomes. Older women (between 38 and 47 years old) contributed
less to the total family income than younger women. Older unmarried
women may represent a more heterogeneous group than younger
unmarried women (more divorcees and widows) and may receive
income from a wider variety of sources.

Unmarried women, like married women, contribute more to yearly
family income as their attachment to the labor force becomes stronger. Eighty percent of the unmarried women who worked for ten
years contributed more than 20 percent of the total family income
(data in Appendix Table C.13). Of those single women working two or
three years out of ten, only 37 percent contributed more than 20
percent of the yearly family income over the number of years they

worked. Looking at the single women who contributed over 75 percent of the yearly family income, we see that 26 percent who worked all ten years earned most of the total family income, whereas only 3 percent of the women who worked two or three years contributed significantly to the family earnings in those years.

Women's Occupations and Earnings

Despite recent increases in labor force participation, in full-time work status, and in women's income, the contributions of wives to husband/wife family earnings do not match the husbands' contributions. The income of both female-headed families and women living alone is also lower than that of men. One reason is that many women work part-time, part-year, and intermittently over a period of years.

A second reason for lower earnings has to do with the occupations that women tend to go into and the pay scales of those occupations. Table 3.7 shows the occupational distribution of working women and mean earnings by occupation. In 1978 the largest proportions of women were clerical workers, service workers, operatives, and professionals. More detailed occupational categories show even more clearly that women are concentrated in a relatively small number of occupations. Interestingly, the occupations of women have not changed much since 1960. Women go into secretarial and clerical work, light factory assembly work, retail sales, services, and certain of the professions—particularly teaching, nursing, and social work.

Table 3.7 also shows the mean earnings in 1977 for women workers by occupation and compares the mean earnings of male and female year-round full-time workers. The mean earnings of female workers stand at about 56 percent of those of males, a rate that has been surprisingly constant over time. In 1955 the median earnings of year-round full-time female workers were about 64 percent of males, 60 percent in 1965, and 59 percent in 1975. The ratio of female to male earnings has, if anything, declined slightly over time.[8]

Like so many other patterns we have examined in this report, the ratio of female to male earnings varies by age. Figure 3.13 shows the ratio for year-round full-time workers by age groups in 1977. The ratio is highest for women in their 20s, falls during their 30s and early 40s, then rises again in their late 40s and 50s. While women's earnings do not rise as rapidly as men's as they move from youth to middle age, neither do they fall as rapidly during the older ages.

Table 3.7. Profile of Women's Labor Force, 1960–1978

Type of Job	Occupational Distribution 1960	Occupational Distribution 1978	Women as % of Workers 1978	Mean Earnings Women 1977	Mean Earnings Full-Time, Year-Round Women Workers 1977	Mean Earnings Full-Time, Year-Round Men Workers 1977
Professional Technical	12.2%	15.6%	42.7%	$8,991	$12,350	$21,320
Managerial-Administrative	5.0	6.1	23.4	8,205	10,329	20,633
Sales	7.6	6.9	44.8	3,933	8,006	18,646
Clerical	29.9	34.6	79.6	6,239	8,937	14,314
Craft	1.0	1.8	5.6	6,499	9,838	14,838
Operatives	15.0	11.8	31.7	5,310	7,659	13,120
Non-Farm Laborers	0.4	1.3	10.4	4,425	7,933	11,133
Service Workers	14.7	17.7	59.1	3,609	6,576	11,181
Private Household	9.8	2.9	97.7	1,479	3,150	—
Farm	4.5	1.3	18.2	1,418	1,741	7,832
Total	100.0%	100.0%	41.2%	$5,826	$ 9,133	$16,171

SOURCE: *Current Population Reports*, "Money Income in 1977 of Families and Persons in the United States, 1979," series P-60, no. 118 (1979).

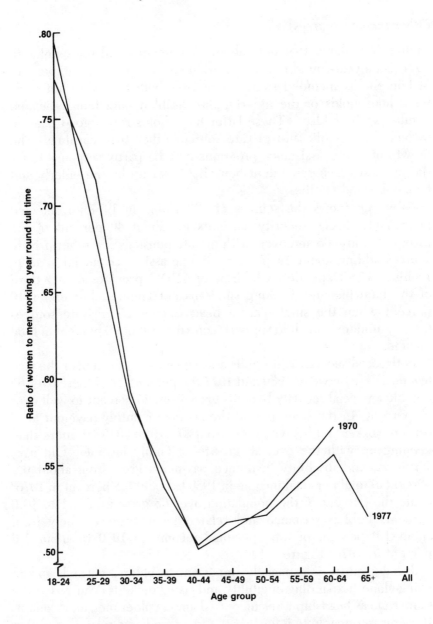

Figure 3.13. Ratio of Earnings of Employed Women to Earnings of Employed Men, 1970 and 1977. *(Source: Appendix Table C. 14.)*

Other Income Sources

Figure 3.10 shows that only about 54 percent of all households in 1977 had a year-round full-time working head. The other 46 percent of households included some young able-bodied adults, but most were households of the elderly, the disabled, and female-headed families with children. These latter households rely a good deal on income from public and private sources other than earnings. The growth of public assistance programs may be partly responsible for the increases in independent households set up by the elderly and female-headed families.

Table 3.8 shows the sources of all income in 1977 for selected households. Social security accounts for about 40 percent of the income of those 65 and over, with private pensions and other private sources adding about 14 percent. Public assistance (mainly Aid to Families with Dependent Children, or AFDC) provides about a third of the total income of young single-parent families, but under 10 percent when the single-parent head is over 25. Private sources (mainly alimony and child support) contribute about 9 percent of total income.

Both social security and public assistance have grown over the past few decades. Between 1950 and 1977 the percentage of those over 65 eligible for social security benefits grew from 25 percent to well over 90 percent. In the same period the average monthly payment for a retired worker and his wife grew from $71.70 to $373.10, more than keeping up with the over-all growth in family income.[9] Old age, survivors, and disability insurance payments grew from about 0.4 percent of total personal income in 1950 to about 5.8 percent in 1976, while the percent of the population over 65 grew from 8.1 to 10.6 percent. Public assistance and related payments grew only from about 1.0 percent of total personal income in 1950 to about 1.6 percent in 1976 (Figure 3.14).

Social security is especially important to older men and women living alone. Expanding eligibility and rising benefits occurred at the same time as headship rates increased among older men and women. It seems reasonable to infer that the two trends are related, and that the expansion of public assistance provided the financial backing that enabled older men and women to establish independent living arrangements. AFDC and other public payments have affected the headship rates of single-parent families in a similar fashion. Although public assistance is only a small proportion of the income of single-parent families in general, it is quite important to young women. The

Table 3.8. Proportion of Aggregate Income from Various Sources, 1977

Household Type	Total	Earnings	Income Other than Earnings				Mean Income	N
			Social Security	Public Assistance & SSI	Dividends, Interest, & Rent	Private Pensions, Alimony, etc.		
Households with Head over 65								
Husband-Wife Households	100.0	33.1	33.9	2.4	16.7	14.0	$12,604	7,048
Male Unrelated Individuals	100.0	19.1	41.6	5.3	16.6	17.3	6,104	1,539
Female Unrelated Individuals	100.0	10.2	48.5	4.5	23.5	13.3	5,101	5,680
Female-Headed Families								
Head <25	100.0	60.6	3.3	28.5	0.2	7.4	4,853	795
Head 25–64	100.0	69.9	7.3	10.6	4.3	8.0	10,079	6,277
Head 65+	100.0	46.3	26.4	5.9	13.3	8.1	11,743	1,164

SOURCE: *Current Population Reports*, "Characteristics of the Population below the Poverty Level: 1977," series P-60, no. 119 (March 1979), Table 38. The category "Husband-Wife Households" also includes a small number of male-headed families.

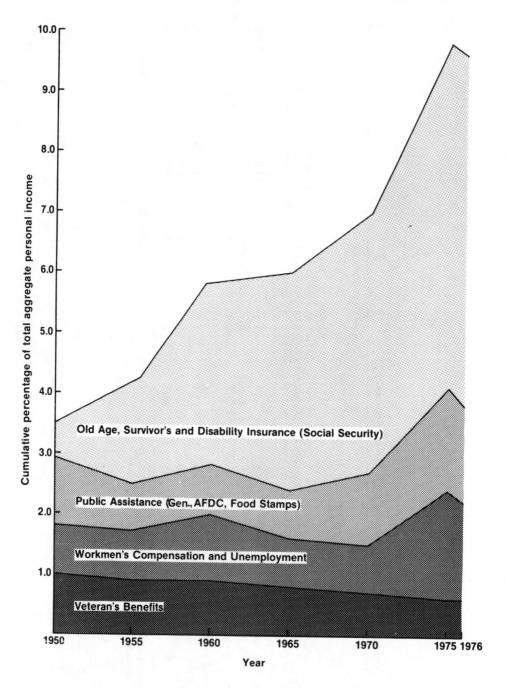

Figure 3.14.   Transfers as a Percentage of Aggregate Personal Income, 1950–1976. *(Source: Appendix Table C. 15.)*

availability of public assistance, if only as a transitional source of income, ensures the financial base that makes it possible for single, divorced, and separated women with children to head their own households.

Because of changes since 1960 in the headship rates of older men and women and of single and previously married women with children, changes in average income of those household types are difficult to interpret. What is clear is that the relative rates of expansion of government transfer programs go hand-in-hand with changes in the poverty rates for various population groups since 1960 (see Figures 3.14 and 3.15). Poverty rates for those 65 and over in 1977 were about 40 percent of their 1959 levels, indicating a substantial rise in over-all standard of living for older people. Poverty rates for female-headed families fell less dramatically; 1977 rates were about 65 percent of 1959 levels. Evidently social security has effectively moved older people out of poverty, while public assistance and other sources of income for female-headed families have been less effective.

Today almost all elderly people live in independent households and almost all are covered by social security. Any changes in the relative income of non-working households, therefore, are likely to arise simply from changes in the levels of public benefits and in changes in the other sources of income available to those who are not full-time workers. Social security benefits are now indexed by law to the Consumer Price Index and are likely to remain at about 40 percent of previous wages for the average worker. Private pensions may expand to fill some of the income gap for older people, but in 1977 they accounted for only about 14 percent of the aggregate income of those over 65. Earnings from part-time work will probably continue to be, as they are now, an important source of income for the elderly. We would expect, though, to continue to see a substantial income gap between the households of older people and those of year-round full-time workers. We would also expect the proportion of the elderly in poverty not to move above the poverty rate for other population groups because of the income floor guaranteed by social security.

Trends in public assistance are harder to predict. Welfare is certainly more controversial than social security and more likely to be cut back during times of government budget tightening. This may lead to more doubling up by some single-parent families, or—continuing a trend that is already evident—more reliance on earnings. Whatever happens, the gap between single-parent and two-parent families is likely to remain large.

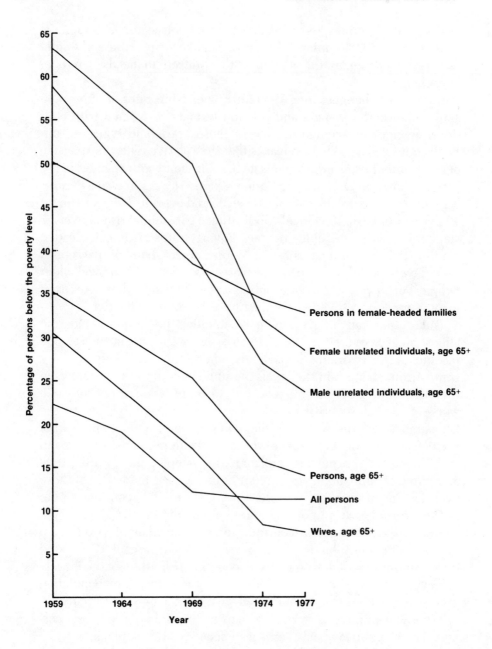

Figure 3.15.   Poverty Rates, 1959–1977. *(Source: Appendix Table C. 16.)*

Income Differentials in 1990

Although the distribution of households is likely to look quite different by 1990, there is not much reason to expect that the substantial income differences between types of households will change much. Women's earnings as a percentage of men's are increasing slowly, if at all. The incomes of two-worker families and of working single-parent (female) families relative to one-worker husband/wife families are likely to increase somewhat because of increased work hours by women, but not because of women's increased wages. We expect the gap to widen slowly between one- and two-worker husband/wife families and to narrow slowly between female-headed and husband/wife families and between working men and women living alone.

Social security income relative to wages is likely to increase somewhat over the next few years as more and more social security recipients are eligible for full benefits, and then to level off. The future of public assistance is much less certain. We would expect to see a slowly narrowing income gap between non-working and working elderly households, and a widening gap between working and non-working households and between one- and two-worker households of other ages.

Notes

1. U.S. Department of Labor, Bureau of Labor Statistics, "Employment and Earnings," vol. 27:1 (Washington, D.C.: GPO, January 1980), Table A-2.
2. Ibid., Tables 2 and 4.
3. Population pyramids represent pictorially the employment and unemployment rates for the total population for 1950, 1960, 1970, and 1978. Population pyramids are based on data presented in Appendix C.
4. Labor force participation rates of men and women from 1950 to 1978 are shown in Appendix Table C.2.
5. Valerie K. Oppenheimer, "The Easterlin Hypotheses: Another Aspect of the Echo to Consider," *Population and Development Review* 2:3&4 (1976), 433–457; Myra H. Strober, "Wives' Labor Force Behavior and Family Consumption Patterns," *American Economic Review* 67:1 (1977), 410–417; Jacob Mincer, "Labor Force Participation of Married Women," *Aspects of Labor Economics*, National Bureau of Economic Research Special Conference Series no. 14 (Princeton: Princeton University Press, 1962), pp. 63–97; Glen G. Cain and Martin D. Dooley, "Estimation of a Model of Labor Supply, Fertility, and Wages of Married Women," *Journal of Political Economy* 84:4, pt. 2 (1976), S179–S199.
6. Permanent attachment to the labor force, defined as working at least seven years out of ten, characterizes about half of 18- to 47-year-old married women and shows no sign of declining.

7. U.S. Dept. of Commerce, Bureau of the Census, *Current Population Reports,* "Consumer Income: 1977," series P-60, no. 118 (March 1979), Table 28.
8. Department of Labor, U.S. Department of Labor Bulletin, *U.S. Working Women: A Databook* (1977), Table 37.
9. In 1950, the average social security benefit was equal to about 26 percent of median family income. In 1977 it was about 30 percent. See Annual Statistical Supplement 1976, *Social Security Bulletin;* and Social Security Administration, Washington, D.C. unpublished data (1980).

Chapter 4

CHANGING FAMILIES,
CHANGING TIMES

Diversity in living arrangements, both in the experiences of men and women over their life courses and in the makeup of households at given points in time, will continue to mark the next decade. The once typical household—two parents and children, with a husband-breadwinner and a wife-homemaker—has faded in prominence. Although most Americans still live in conventional nuclear families sometime during their lives, traditional families are a small minority of all households at any given time. Other types of households—two-worker families, families whose children have moved away, retired couples, single-parent families, and men and women living alone—are proliferating and are becoming an increasing proportion of households overall.

The phenomenon of more and more individuals spending less and less time in traditional family living arrangements has provoked a good deal of anxiety on several counts. First, families and family relationships in our society have long been considered major elements of a meaningful life. If fewer and fewer people live in families, the argument goes, this source of meaning and satisfaction may be lost, leaving many people disoriented and alienated. Second, families have long sheltered and cared for society's dependent members: children, the elderly, the sick, the disabled, and the poor. Changes in the family lead to questions about who will take on this care: Will children be raised to be healthy, productive, and moral adults? Will the old and sick be treated with dignity and compassion? Third, families have provided an element of stability to the economy, historically generating predictable demands for goods and services, and supplying the labor market with reliable sources of workers. Changes in family workers, income, and consumption choices introduce a large element of uncertainty into all of this, a concern to business and government planners.

Whether these concerns and anxieties turn out to be justified or not depends on how individuals, families, and other institutions react and adapt to the changes. People may—but need not—find new types of family ties and satisfying friendships that cross household boundaries. New ways of caring for dependents may—or may not—evolve within families and through the cooperation of marketplace and government institutions with families. Households may develop new life styles, with work and consumption patterns different from the idealized suburban pattern.

We expect changes in households and families to be accompanied by new relationships within families and among households, the community, the economy, and the government. Our discussion is frankly speculative because we know very little about how these new relationships are developing. Nonetheless, we will touch on a number of profoundly important issues that are emerging. We will also propose some hypotheses for thought and future research about three general questions:

1. Where are adults likely to look for and find satisfying personal relationships to complement or replace those traditionally found in family households?
2. What new life styles are likely to develop in terms of housing choices and the purchase of goods and services to reflect the new time and resource constraints facing many households?
3. What new demands are likely to be made on government for both income and services?

Personal Relationships

Many observers raise questions about whether the increasing numbers of one- and two-person households will lead to a society in which large numbers of people are essentially alone and cut off from others. The answer depends on the extent and quality of relationships outside the household with family, friends, neighbors, and others. These relationships are not well understood at least partly because most statistical sources focus only on relationships within households.

For most people during the next decade there will be more opportunities for cross-household family relationships. Based on current life expectancies, most people will have living parents until they are well into their 40s. Thus the young and middle-aged men and women who live alone or in single-parent households (as well as married people) have a long period of their adult lives to maintain relationships with their parents. Most of these people will also have at least one brother or sister, while young adults of the baby boom generation will have several siblings. When children born in the 1970s reach young adulthood, they will have, on the average, fewer brothers and sisters, but they are just as likely to have living parents and stepparents.

A small proportion of older adults have living parents or living brothers and sisters. Many, however, have living children. About three-quarters of the women currently 65 and over had at least one child, and a significant number of these children are still surviving. In the next generation of elderly (the parents of the baby boom), almost 90 percent of the women will have had at least one child and most will have had several children. Even if elderly men and women of that generation choose to live alone, as seems likely, the possibility of their maintaining family ties exists.

Whether cross-household family ties actually are maintained depends on several things, including geography, available time, and personal preference. Two-worker and single-parent families in their middle years, for example, are likely to be quite pressed for time, which may severely constrain their ability to spend much time with elderly parents or brothers and sisters. The important point is that despite changing household patterns, almost everyone lives in a family during childhood and most people live in family households at other times in their lives as well. They establish family relationships that can persist despite changes in households.

The decreased size of families and the difficulties in many cases of maintaining family ties may, however, increase the importance of friendship, neighborhoods, and organizations as sources of social support and of personal ties. Roommates and partners already provide young, unrelated individuals with substitutes for familial relationships. These friendships often resemble family relationships in their intensity and intimacy and in the needs that are met (economic, sexual, social, emotional), but they differ in the breadth and endurance of commitment. Because such ties are not embedded in a large and relatively stable kinship network, they are more easily suspended.

In addition, people who live alone may seek out places to live and work where they expect others to share their interests and circumstances. Retirement communities, "singles" apartment complexes, and urban neighborhoods may be the basis of social life for groups of relatively homogeneous households.

Surveys on the amount of contact that people have with family, friends, and neighbors and on their membership in organizations find almost no completely isolated individuals. (There might be some, of course, who are isolated from surveys as well.) Most people in all household types report a good deal of social activity.[1] Unmarried men, especially older men, may be an exception; they seem often to be quite alone. There are no historical data available for comparison, however, and even the existing data are hard to interpret. This is clearly an area in which new research is needed.

New Life Styles

However valid it may have been in the 1960s to identify the suburban nuclear-family life style as characteristic of the society, it is certainly not valid in the 1980s. That life style meant families with children, male workers, and female homemakers—a household type that is not only an increasingly small proportion of all households but one in which individual adults will spend even less time in the future. The life styles of two-worker families, single parents, and men and women living alone are likely to differ from traditional family life styles in important ways and to be fundamentally different from each other in their use of money and time.

Two-Worker Families

Two-worker families are likely to have more money and less time than demographically similar one-worker families. Assuming that other family members do not reduce their work hours or earnings when wives work (which on the whole they do not), family income increases by the amount of the wives' earnings. The simple fact of wives' spending a certain number of hours in the paid labor force reduces the hours available to the women or their families for alternative uses. How much more money and how much less time for families, however, depends on how much wives work and how much they earn. We would expect the answers to these questions to lead, in turn, to differences in consumption patterns among families, in the time allocated to household tasks, in leisure activities among family members, and in the choice of where to live.

Consumption of Goods and Services.   A few studies on consumer expenditures have examined the spending patterns of one- and two-worker families and have found remarkably few differences. With the exception of work-related expenses for the additional worker, the spending patterns of two-worker families were basically similar to those of one-worker families.[2]

In a smaller but more detailed study, the effects of working wives on family consumption patterns depended on the income level of the families, on the extent to which wives' jobs were permanent and substantial and on life-style preferences.[3] Unless the wives had a long history of substantial work experience, families made basic life-style decisions (for example, on type, quality, and location of housing) on the basis of husbands' earnings alone. The temporary income of wives went for extras like home furnishings, clothes, or travel.

Consistent with these spending patterns is our hypothesis that changes in consumption depend on the extent of wives' attachment to the labor force. At low levels of attachment, where the wife's work is intermittent and her earnings are modest, we would expect very few changes in family spending patterns.

At medium levels of attachment, where wives' earnings are more predictable but neither large nor permanent, we would expect to see wives' income earmarked for large but one-time expenses such as down payment on housing, children's college expenses, major appliances, furniture, vacations, or investments. Wives' earnings might also be taken into account in qualifying for a mortgage in terms of the monthly payments that the bank feels the family could afford. These wives may become trapped in the labor force and committed to more permanent work than they prefer, which in turn may influence the family's decisions about having children or making other family commitments.

With the possible exception of contributions toward housing, the earnings of moderately attached wives would normally be treated as transitory rather than permanent income. The families' basic level of consumption and their choices of goods and services would remain relatively constant over time. The wives' temporary income would show up in savings and perhaps in one-time purchases.

When wives' earnings are substantial and permanent, reflecting a high level of attachment, we would expect to see them making an important difference in family life styles. We would expect those earnings, for example, to be a more reliable and important element in housing decisions and to be realistically entered into the family budget for monthly mortgage payments as well as down payments. We would also expect to see more spending on time-saving goods and services, with wives' work both permitting and requiring the sub-stitution of money for time on such activities as meal preparation, housekeeping, and perhaps leisure.

If our interpretation is correct, it is not surprising that substantially different consumption patterns are not apparent in either research studies or everyday life. We know that although large proportions of wives work, only a small proportion of them work year-round full-time over a period of years. If the establishment of new consumption patterns occurs only when wives are strongly attached workers, we would expect to see them only among that small minority of families in the middle and older generations where the wives are indeed career women.

With more younger generation wives becoming more attached to jobs, which we believe is happening, the next decade may see some quite important shifts as the cohorts born after 1940 move through their life course. These cohorts appear to be establishing, in their 20s and 30s, patterns of delayed marriage, higher household headship, lower fertility, and higher divorce—patterns not unrelated to their greater attachment to the labor force. They may not be "settling down" in marriage and parenting as fast as earlier cohorts, if at all; they may be developing life styles characterized by less permanency and less attachment to the conventional accoutrements of nuclear-family living. Although they do seem to be buying homes at younger ages, even while unmarried, they may be viewing them more as investments than as a commitment to a life style.[4]

Time and Task Allocation.   Most recent research on time use and task allocation within households also shows relatively minor differ-ences between one-worker and two-worker families. According to most studies, for example, working wives continue to do most of the cooking, housework, and child care for their families.[5] They do spend less time on housework and child care than non-working wives do. A 1975 urban time use study found that working wives spent an average of about 25 hours a week on "family care" while non-working wives spent about 44.[6] The difference seems to represent work foregone rather than work reallocated to other household members. Several studies have shown that husbands of working wives do not spend significantly more time on housework and child care than husbands of non-working wives.[7]

A study comparing differences in time use in 1965 and 1975 found that employed wives in 1965 had much longer working days—that is, work for pay plus family care—than employed husbands or housewives. In 1965 employed women worked 67.2 hours a week, employed men 60.3, and housewives 50. The study found employed wives in 1975 and employed husbands much more similar in total work hours, at 55 and 57 hours a week, respectively. (Housewives worked 45 hours.) Employed wives reduced the amount of time spent on family care by about 4 hours, from 29 hours a week in 1965 to 25 hours in 1975. (The study reports, interestingly, that the reduction came almost entirely in housework rather than in child care.) Employed husbands only increased the time they spent on family care by about 42 minutes, from 9 to 9.7 hours a week.[8]

These findings over time are consistent with the suggestion that younger cohorts may be developing somewhat different life styles than older generations. In 1965 most women who worked would have been born before 1940, members of the generation that produced the baby boom and was subject to a societal emphasis on home and family. When these women went back to work, they might have felt compelled to keep up the housekeeping and family care standards they developed when they were young wives and mothers. They did this by extending their own work days, adding hours of paid work onto almost full-time housework.

By 1975 more women born after 1940 would have moved into the ranks of employed women. Although they worked at paid jobs no more hours than women in 1965, they reduced their time on family care considerably. Their lower fertility rates probably contributed to this change, but a substantial reduction in housework unrelated to children also seems to have taken place. It may be that these younger women are doing housework more efficiently, perhaps relying on labor-saving appliances or paid help. It may also be that they are developing different and less demanding standards of home upkeep.

The change between 1965 and 1975 is best described as a reduction in housework rather than a reallocation; employed men increased their family care time by much less than employed women decreased theirs. Negotiating the sharing of housework may be more difficult than deciding to decrease it. Nonetheless, we may be seeing some reallocation of household tasks, and may see more as wives continue to increase their labor force participation and attachment.

We hypothesize that changes in patterns of time use, like changes in consumption patterns, depend on wives' attachment to the labor force rather than simply on participation. At low levels of attachment, we would expect only marginal changes in families' use of time and division of tasks. We would expect some reductions in housework, some assumption of tasks by husbands, perhaps some reductions in sleep and leisure time of wives, and perhaps some increase in the purchase of services. We might expect to see some evidence of strain on families produced by time pressures but no substantial renegotiation or change in families' conceptions of who should do what.

At medium levels of wives' work attachment we might expect greater time pressures on families and a greater need to share tasks more equally. The actual outcome would probably be influenced by the amount of family work to be done, particularly whether or not there are young children, and by wives' and husbands' perceptions of appropriate male and female roles. At one extreme, a family without young children and an egalitarian ideology might experience an amicable division of tasks among the wife, the husband, and perhaps paid help. Potential problems exist in other situations at the other extreme. A traditional ideology in a family with young children, for example, could easily lead to severe overburdening of the wife and to disagreements over who should do what. If a family had only older children and if the husband and wife shared a traditional sex-role ideology, the wife might make nearly all the necessary adaptations. She might continue to do most of the housework and take time for paid work from what might have been extra daytime leisure.

When wives have high levels of work attachment, we would expect to see even more change toward an egalitarian division of tasks and perhaps in some families even more conflict between husband and wife. We would also expect to see significant substitutions of money for time: paid housework and child care services, labor-saving household appliances, convenience foods, and the like.

As with consumption, if our hypotheses are correct it is not surprising that general surveys of time use and task allocation do not find important differences between one-worker and two-worker families. Because we would expect substantial time-use changes to accompany only substantial attachment, and since we know that attachment on the average is low among wives over the age of 35 in 1980, gross comparisons of working and non-working wives are not likely to be particularly revealing. Studies that distinguished among the three generations would tell us more.

Choice of Where to Live. During the late 1960s and early 1970s, the geographic distribution of the population began to shift. Many rural, small town, and central city areas began to gain population after decades of loss to suburban areas. Young adults in the prime marriage and childbearing years (age 25–34) began moving to or remaining in the central cities, while older adults age 35–64 moved out. By 1977 the age group 25–34 represented about 16 percent of the total population of both central cities and suburbs; however, the marriage and fertility levels of the central city group were much lower. Because of the over-all decline in fertility between 1970 and 1977, both central city and suburban areas saw a decline in the percentage of children under 14 years of age, but the central city decline was twice that of the suburbs (20 percent compared to 10 percent).

The number of family-occupied central city households declined slightly during the 1970s, while the number maintained by persons living alone or living only with non-relatives increased by 31 percent between 1970 and 1977. Widows accounted for a significant fraction of this latter trend, but the contribution of young adults was also substantial.

The age of family heads living in suburban areas rose, on the average, during the period 1970 to 1977. The proportion under age 25 declined while their counterparts in both central city and nonmetropolitan areas increased.

The $15,000 mean income of families who moved into central cities between 1975 and 1977 was about $1,000 lower than the mean of families who moved out. Although the income ratio for the new urban dwellers improves substantially when adjustments are made for age and family size, nonmetropolitan areas showed the largest gains in family income during 1969–1976. Over this seven-year period, the number of college graduates living in central cities increased by 45 percent compared with a 42 percent increase both in suburbs and nonmetropolitan areas—an indication that new urban households will differ in earning power from those of the recent past.

The trends in decisions about where to live have not been categorized by the number of earners in the household. We can speculate, however, that two-earner couples with children would probably attempt to balance the employment, cultural, and transportation advantages of central city living against housing and educational advantages of suburban living. Families with more and older children would opt to live outside of central cities, while childless couples and those with one or two children would be more likely to see advantages in living "in town."[9]

We do know that in 1977 the over-all labor force participation rate of women was slightly higher in the suburbs than in the central cities, a reversal from 1970. The changed age composition of both areas probably accounts for the shift; the cities have gained a larger proportion of both younger women (age 18–24) and women over 65. For women age 25–54 participation was higher in the central cities than in the suburbs, giving some support to the hypothesis that central cities may attract two-worker and other working-women households.

Geographical mobility patterns for families with one and two workers show some differences. Between 1975 and 1978, for example, married women who were in the labor force in 1978 were more likely to have moved within counties and less likely to have moved between states than women not in the labor force. The differences, however, were small. Of 35- to 44-year-old married women workers in 1978, 14.9 percent had moved within counties and 4.3 percent had moved between states. Of those not in the labor force, 12.1 percent had moved within counties and 7.3 percent had moved between states.

While it is possible that labor force participation is determined by mobility rather than vice versa, there are reasons to expect working wives to have higher within-county and lower between-state mobility than non-working wives. In what is becoming a familiar refrain, we would expect the degree of difference to be related to wives' degree of attachment to the labor force.

Theoretically at least, two-worker families would be more likely than one-worker families to move to better housing, reflecting their increased income. They might also be more likely to move to ease the time-constraint problems of two workers in getting to work, shopping, chauffeuring children, purchasing services, and having access to recreational activities. At the same time, long-distance moves would be less likely because of the difficulties in finding jobs for two people in the same area.

These decisions about where to live are likely to be much more important for wives with strong labor force commitments. Women with part-time or intermittent jobs would not feel the same degree of time pressure. Nor are they likely to consider their own career or job prospects an obstacle to job-related moves by their husbands. Strongly attached working wives, on the other hand, are more likely to favor residential moves that would decrease commuting, shopping, and other traveling time. At the same time, career women would be less likely to favor long-distance moves that would jeopardize their marriages or their own spouse's prospects of having a satisfying job.

As women become increasingly attached to the labor force, we expect that two-worker families will develop life styles that reflect their having relatively more money and relatively less time than one-worker families. They might be expected to look for more convenient housing, to invest in time-saving goods, and to purchase more services. They might be more interested in leisure activities that can be done at home, or in housing convenient to recreational facilities, especially when they are childless. They may, in sum, demand different kinds of houses, goods, and services than one-worker families.

Single-Parent Families

Single-parent families, which are predominantly women with children, are likely to have less money and less time than two-parent families with the same number of children simply because there is one less adult in the household. In some low income families the husband may have spent more on himself than he earned, or required more care-taking time than he contributed. In such families the woman and children may find themselves with more money or more time after the separation than before. Although there are exceptions, on average, we expect these families to be pressed for both time and money.

Adjustment to Lower Income. Few data are available on how single-parent families in different generations adjust their consumption to fit their sudden drop in income. An obvious candidate for cutbacks is housing because it is a major item in most families' budgets and because single-parent families can presumably get along with smaller, less expensive housing than two-parent families. When we looked at what families reported they spent on housing, however, we found little difference between housing costs when married and housing costs after the break. While some women decreased their spending on housing, others increased theirs; the result was thus little net change. Housing costs as a percentage of income, of course, increased substantially after the break.[10]

With lower incomes and housing costs remaining constant, single-parent families must spend less on other items. They spend considerably less on food.[11] They probably save less and may often, in fact, spend from previous savings or got into debt. They probably spend less on recreation, clothing, and other discretionary items. How much they spend on work-related expenses, the largest of which tends to be child care, depends on whether they work (about 70 percent do) and how much they work. Depending on the magnitude of the drop in their income (see Figure 3.11), the consumption

adjustment of single-parent families may be substantial. How painful
the adjustments are may depend on the extent to which the basic life
style established during the marriage can be maintained. The pain
may also depend on whether the single-parent state is experienced
and perceived as temporary or permanent. A large majority of single
mothers do remarry, many of them within a relatively short time. For
these transitional families, consumption adjustments may take the
form of deferring purchases rather than adjusting to a lower basic
standard of living.

The consumption patterns of single-parent families may reflect the
sources as well as the level of their income. An important distinction
may be whether income is reliable or irregular. Single-parent families, as noted in Chapter 3, receive income from private and public
transfers as well as from their own earnings. None of these income
sources may be particularly reliable. Attachment may be higher for
single parents than for wives, but even unmarried women show
considerable movement in and out of the labor force. The combination of child-care responsibilities and unstable employment may
make it difficult for a woman to count on adequate earnings over long
periods of time. Alimony and child support payments may be even
less regular. Court awards tend to be small and are by no means
universally honored.[12]

Social security is a stable and important source of income for
widows, and most of them rely on survivors' benefits as an income
base while they have dependent children.[13] Public assistance (usually
Aid to Families with Dependent Children and Food Stamps) is less
adequate and is used as an income source by a smaller proportion of
the eligible population than that which collects social security. (Public
assistance accounts for less than 10 percent of income among female-
headed families generally.) Eligibility is reassessed periodically, and
since application and reassessment require visits to welfare offices
that can be difficult and demeaning, many single parents look on
public assistance as an unreliable or as a voluntarily temporary income source.[14]

The question of how single-parent families adjust spending and
consumption patterns when one or more of their income sources are
transitory is as yet unanswered. It would seem unreasonable for them
to base consumption on current uncertain income. Perhaps some
women judge their "normal" income to be what they had in the past
and expect in future marriages. Perhaps others come to see their own
earnings or earnings potential as providing their permanent income

and define their standards of living accordingly. Others may adjust their spending on a short-term, month-to-month basis.

Labor force attachment would be expected to be an important dimension of how income is viewed. Strongly attached women working year-round and full-time in secure jobs with promotion opportunities would expect to have substantially higher earnings than other single-parent families. They would also, we think, be more likely to see their primary long-term levels of income coming from their own earnings. They would base their consumption decisions and their aspirations for their standard of living on their expectations about future earnings. They would be more likely to make long-term plans such as buying a house in a location and of a type that they could pay for themselves. Perhaps they would tend to adjust their standard of living down to their earnings rather than to use savings or debt in an attempt to keep up what they had when they were married.

We expect attachment to work to increase among women who head families. As a result, we expect them to have higher incomes and more stable consumption patterns, probably including higher rates of home ownership. We would also expect less reliance on public assistance, and perhaps more reliance on advancing their education, on vocational training, and on job placement programs. All this should lead to a greater sense of well-being (if level and permanency of income are related to well-being as they seem to be) and perhaps to less incentive for quick remarriage. If these hypotheses are correct, we may see more stable, better defined, and higher standards of living among single-parent families in the future.

Time and Task Allocation. Single-parent families, like two-parent families, spend time in paid work and on family and child care, as well as on personal care, socializing with friends and relatives, sleep, recreation, and leisure. Two sets of decisions basically define how single-parent families cope with the demands on their time: decisions about working by the single parent and decisions about the number and allocation of household tasks to be performed.

Most single parents work, but only about half currently work year-round full-time. Full-time work means higher income, but less time for children, housework, and so on. Mothers of young children tend to disagree on whether the income gain is worth the time loss or worth arranging for substantial child care.[15] Like working wives, working single parents can cope with household tasks by reducing them, hiring help, or reallocating them within the family. The possibilities for reallocation are, of course, less than in two-parent families, but children in single-parent families do seem to be asked to do more chores.

Choice of Where to Live. When a couple splits up, the usual presumption is that the husband moves out and the wife and children stay where they had been living. This seems to be what happens immediately following most marital disruptions, but the wife and children do not stay put for long. Our analyses show very high levels of residential mobility in the first few years after divorce or separation, but not after being widowed. Many single-parent families move several times in the course of two or three years.[16]

Where and why they move is less clear. Female-headed families are more likely than husband/wife families to live in metropolitan areas and, within those, to live in large central cities.[17] Like other families, however, when they move they are more likely to move from central cities than to them. We found no unambiguous patterns of moves to smaller or larger quarters, or to cheaper housing. Substantially more single parents switched from owning to renting than from renting to owning.[18] Our impressions from interview data are that financial considerations force many moves; other moves are made to get away from the married home; and still others are made to have more convenient or satisfying quarters. Single parents seem to feel both a desire to provide neighborhood and school continuity for their children, and a desire to make their own lives more pleasant by relocating within reach of work, friends, or recreational opportunities. Their high mobility may reflect the difficulty of satsifying competing demands on limited budgets.[19]

We would expect work attachment to be related to housing decisions and therefore to mobility. We have no evidence on which to base clear predictions, however. It will be interesting to see whether single-parent families do begin to show greater work attachment and whether such attachment is then followed by increased home ownership or by housing and mobility decisions tied to job considerations.

Men and Women Living Alone

The categories of men and women living alone include people of very different ages. They are disproportionately young and old, in contrast to two-worker and single-parent families which tend to be adults in the 25- to 64-year age range. Their patterns of consumption, time use, and mobility are as likely to be defined as much by age as by household type or work status.

Young men and women who live alone tend to be working, though some of them are students. They have relatively low earnings but expectations of higher earnings in the future. They tend to move often, to rent rather than own, and to have quite flexible life styles.[20] More than any other household type, they live in central cities. Their marital status for past cohorts has tended to be temporary, since most of them married or remarried relatively quickly. If, as we have projected, more in the future will stay unmarried longer, young unmarried men and women may begin to have more stable life styles. They may show some of the signs of settling down, perhaps buying homes, moving less, and investing both time and money in their homes.

Men and women over 65 who live alone tend not to be employed. They have relatively low incomes (a substantial portion of which comes from social security), low residential mobility, and high rates of home ownership.[21] They tend to live disproportionately in central cities and nonmetropolitan areas and are less likely to live in the suburbs. We do not know the extent to which this may change— whether, for example, more will move to retirement communities. Our discussion of personal relationships suggested why retirement communities might become more popular. The new capital-gains tax provisions that make it less costly for the elderly to sell their homes may also encourage more moves. If the elderly moved into housing developed for families with children when they themselves were young, they may find themselves in relatively homogeneous communities simply by staying put in their own homes. Or they may decide that mixed-age communities provide more diverse and satisfying personal relationships and stay in more mobile communities for that reason. Whatever decisions the elderly make on housing, and whatever social and economic forces affect these decisions, they are bound to have important effects on the shape and feel of communities and on the availability of housing for other groups.

Families and Government

Providing care, support, and shelter for the young, the old, the sick, the disabled, and the poor is one of the most important tasks that families have provided for society. If more and more people are expected to live outside families, how will this care and support be provided? As more women join the paid labor force, are we likely to see a shift in caretaking responsibilities from families to paid outsiders or to public agencies? Are public assistance programs likely to become a more major source of income for the elderly, children, and other dependents?

Income and Service "Packages." A useful way to explore the roles of families, government, and other institutions in caring for dependents is to think in terms of an income or service "package." Families receive income from a variety of sources. One family may rely on the wife's earnings, the husband's earnings, and interest. Another may receive income from the single head's earnings, child support, and food stamps. Yet another's income package may be made up of a couple's social security, private pension, earnings, and help from the children. Family income thus can come from several sources—the market, government, and kin.

In an analogous fashion, different institutions can provide the physical care, help, and support that children, the frail elderly, and other dependents require. Families provide most of the care now as in the past. But nursing and housekeeping help, for example, can also be hired, be given by private charitable groups, or be provided through government agencies. Child care can come from parents, relatives, paid baby sitters, schools, or day-care centers. As with income, families put together service packages; similarly, government can be an important contributor to the packages.

Income. As discussed in Chapter 3, public cash assistance programs have grown since 1950 and are an important income source for the elderly and single-parent families. The most important program is social security, which has broadly based political and popular support. Old Age, Survivors, and Disability Insurance will continue to be an important source of income for the old and disabled, and social security—which has become an accepted part of the income package—will continue to grow as a proportion of total personal income.

Other cash transfer programs for the elderly, the unemployed, and single-parent families are less significant and have not grown substantially as a proportion of personal income. They are politically controversial and are unlikely to expand much over the next decade, particularly as women's work and earnings increase.

Services. Government spending on social welfare services has also expanded since 1950, but, with one exception, is not large. The exception is spending on health and medical care, which increased from 1.2 percent of GNP in 1950 to 3.7 percent of GNP in 1977. In contrast federal, state, and local spending on institutional care, child welfare services, and "other social welfare," which includes day care, programs for the aged, programs for juvenile delinquents, foster care, and some other services went from 0.05 percent of GNP in 1950 to 0.24 percent in 1977—almost a five-fold increase but a relatively small amount of money. Spending on vocational rehabilitation went from 0.01 percent of GNP in 1950 to 0.06 in 1977; on child nutrition from 0.06 percent of GNP in 1950 to 0.18 percent in 1977.[22]

If present trends continue, government may play an increasingly important but still small role in providing care and support services for children, the elderly, and other dependents. Demands for expanded government services may well increase over the next decade as changes take place in families and households.

Surveys depict family members, especially daughters, providing a good deal of help and companionship to the elderly. Adults report that they frequently visit, phone, and exchange letters with their parents. They also report giving various kinds of help such as housework and shopping.[23]

Predicting the future of intergenerational assistance is difficult. A large proportion of today's elderly entered adulthood during the Depression, an experience which affected their family formation patterns (substantial numbers remained unmarried and childless)—and probably their attitudes toward financial and residential independence. Many of their daughters came of age during the post-World War II period. Although these women entered the labor force in large proportions, they also had large families. They may, after raising their own children, carry over their family commitments into feelings of obligation toward aging parents—or they may hurry to escape family responsibilities.

As they become the next generation of elderly, between now and the end of this century, they might look for support to their baby boom children, whose childhood spanned the relative affluence of the 1950s and early 1960s and who entered adulthood in the late 1960s and 1970s. The women in these younger cohorts have much lower marriage and fertility rates and much stronger commitments to careers than their mothers. More of them are likely to spend much of their adult lives in time-pressed two-worker and single-parent families. Relatively less individual sacrifice may be required to provide care and support when their parents need it, however, since there are more children to share the load among the baby boom generation.

Care arrangements for children, like those for the elderly, show a continued reliance on families, with important assistance from schools. Schools now enroll about 99 percent of 6- to 15-year-olds and about 90 percent of 16- to 17-year-olds, percentages that have changed only slightly over the last decade. Dramatic changes have, however, taken place in the school enrollment of 3- to 5-year-olds. Slightly more than a third of 3- to 4-year-olds went to nursery schools in 1978, up from about 14 percent in 1967. About 83 percent of 5-year-olds went to kindergarten in 1978, up from about 68 percent in 1967. (Another 8 percent of 5-year-olds were in first grade.) About a third of those in nursery school and over 80 percent of those in kindergarten were in public programs.[24]

When children are not in school, most are cared for by their parents and some by other relatives. Almost half of the mothers who work report themselves as the primary caretakers of both pre-school and school-age children. Fewer than 20 percent of pre-schoolers are cared for by someone other than their parents for 35 hours or more a week, and most of those are in informal baby sitting or family care arrangements. Less than 10 percent of pre-schoolers use formal day care (exclusive of nursery school) either full or part time.[25]

The next decade may see a greater shift toward non-parental arrangements for the care of children. Women in their 20s are now in the labor force in much larger numbers than previous cohorts of 20- to 29-year-olds, and they seem to be showing a greater commitment to their work careers and a more permanent attachment to the labor force. This cohort of women is marrying late, postponing childbearing, and planning to have very small families. They may put together a new combination of work and family life that uses nursery schools, day-care centers, and paid child-care help more extensively. Continued high divorce rates would reinforce this trend. If present patterns persist, however, most of this child care will be provided informally. There may, on the other hand, be increasing demands on the public schools to provide pre-school care for 3- to 5-year-olds and after-school care for older children.

It seems likely that families in 1990 will be looking to non-family sources for help with the care of children, the elderly, and other dependents. Many of these services—for example, meal preparation and housekeeping for the elderly and nursery school for pre-school children—will be purchased privately, as they are now. Others may become the responsibility of government. The substantial commitment of public funds for income support for the elderly, the disabled, and other dependent groups may, however, preclude much additional spending on services, especially if present attitudes toward government spending persist. Debate over these issues is clearly one of the vital political tasks of the next decade.

Postscript

We have speculated on some of the implications of the concrete changes we have measured and projected in the structure of American households and families. There are many more changes under way that are less obvious in the data but are nonetheless significant. Some of these changes have been alluded to in this report, but in closing we would like to list them as part of an agenda for future research.

Couples who live together but are not married, and reconstituted families with and without children, are thought to be a rapidly growing share of conjugal relationships. Our data, however, treat unmarried persons almost exclusively as individuals and rarely distinguish between first marriages and remarriages or require inferences from data on household membership. These distinctions become important, especially when children are involved. Much attention is directed at children in single-parent households, but are nonresident parents and surrogate parents filling in with significant amounts of child care? Are children clearly better off when a parent remarries? How do children cope with multiple households, many of which are undergoing changes?

The case of two households sharing the same child is only one example of a myriad of important exchanges and interactions between people who live in separate households. Such cross-household interaction is a very important part of the changes in household structure and functioning we have been discussing but for which we have little direct national data. Are people who live alone really "alone" for most of their meals, evenings, and leisure time? Are childless households really free of the presence of children? Do the elderly who live alone receive much support from others outside their household? How do different households combine their separate resources to meet their individual needs?

Unmarried individuals live in more "fluid" living arrangements than married couples, according to some evidence, with more rapid turnover of household members and more frequent housing changes. More detailed evidence of these transitions over time would be useful in interpreting the data we have on diversity in household and family structure at a particular point in time. How long do people stay in single-person households? What is the average number of partners or roommates people live with before they get married? How many different individuals does this involve? How long do children live in single-parent households?

Finally, concerns that should be high on the agenda for future research are the interrelations among various life-course activities and events. Some observers say that we are moving away from the pattern in which fractions of a lifetime are devoted sequentially and almost exclusively first to education, then to single adulthood, then to work (for men) and childrearing (for women), and finally to the leisure of the retirement years. Are these activities increasingly being spread more randomly over the entire life course, with all or most taking place simultaneously at any given time? If such a generalization is true, it has profound implications for the organization of time and other resources in families and households. At this point we know very little about *interactions* between changing life-course variables on a national scale simply because data are collected and reported by a variety of separate statistical agencies.[26] Well designed sample surveys to collect data that examine the integration of the dimensions of the life course are needed before we can reach any real understanding of these interactions.

Notes

1. Claude S. Fischer, R. Jackson, C. A. Steuve, K. Gerson, L. Jones, M. Baldassare, *Networks and Places* (New York: Free Press, 1977), chapters 3 and 4; J. B. Lansing, R. Marans, and R. Zehner, *Planned Residential Environments* (Ann Arbor: Institute for Social Research of the University of Michigan, 1970); W. Michelson, "Environmental Change," *Research Paper* no. 60 (Toronto: Centre for Urban and Community Studies of the University of Toronto, n.d.); C. Alexander, "The City as a Mechanism for Sustaining Human Contact," in *Urbanman*, J. Helmer and N. A. Eddington, eds. (New York: Free Press, 1973).

2. Myrna H. Strober, "Wives' Labor Force Behavior and Family Consumption Patterns," *American Economic Review* 67:1 (1977), 410–417; Myrna H. Strober and Charles B. Weinberg, "Working Wives and Major Family Expenditures," *Journal of Consumer Research* (December 1977), pp. 141–146; Clair Vickery, "The Work of Married Women and the Living Standards of Their Families," in *The Subtle Revolution: Women at Work*, Ralph E. Smith, ed. (Washington, D.C.: The Urban Institute, 1979).

3. Richard P. Coleman, "Husbands, Wives, and Other Earners: Notes on the Family Income Assembly Line," *Working Paper* no. 48 (Cambridge, Mass.: MIT-Harvard Joint Center for Urban Studies, 1978).

4. John R. Pitkin and George Masnick, "Analysis and Projection of Housing Consumption by Birth Cohorts: 1960–2000," a research report prepared by the MIT-Harvard Joint Center for Urban Studies for U.S. Department of Housing and Urban Development Grant #H-2842RG (August 1979).

5. F. Thomas Juster, "The Investment of Time by Households: A Preliminary View" (Paper prepared for the American Statistical Association Meeting, August 1978); John P. Robinson, *How Americans Use Time* (New York: Praeger, 1977); Alexander Szalai, "Women's Time: Women in the Light of Contemporary Time-Budget Research," *Futures* (October 1975), pp. 385–399; Kathryn E. Walker and Margaret E. Woods, *Time Use: A Measure of Household Production of Family Goods and Services* (Washington, D.C.: American Home Economics Association, 1976), Tables 6.4, 6.5, 6.6; John Robinson and E. Rogers-Millar, "Housework, Technology and Quality of Life: Implications from Longitudinal Time-Use Surveys," in *Household Work*, Sarah F. Beck, ed. (Beverly Hills, California: Sage Publications, 1979).

6. John P. Robinson, *Changes in Americans' Use of Time: 1965–1975* (Cleveland: Communication Research Center, 1977), Table 4.

7. Greg Duncan and Frank Stafford, "The Use of Time and Technology in Households in the United States" (Ann Arbor: Survey Research Center of the Institute for Social Research, University of Michigan, n.d.); George Farkas, "Education, Wage Rates, and the Division of Labor between Husband and Wife," *Journal of Marriage and the Family* 38:3 (1976); Kathryn E. Walker and Margaret E. Woods, *Time Use*, p. 144; Joseph Pleck, L. Lang, and M. Rustad, "Men's Family Work, Involvement, and Satisfaction," mimeographed (Wellesley: Wellesley College Center for Research on Women, 1978).

8. John P. Robinson, *Changes in Americans' Use of Time*. Table 4.

9. U.S. Bureau of the Census, *Current Population Reports*, "Social and Economic Characteristics of Metropolitan and Nonmetropolitan Population: 1977 and 1970," series P-23, no. 75 (November 1978).

10. Taken from Panel Study of Income Dynamics computer runs by Susan Bartlett.

11. Taken from Panel Study of Income Dynamics computer runs by Nancy Goodban.

12. *Current Population Reports*, "Divorce, Child Custody and Child Support," series P-23, no. 84 (June 1979).

13. *Current Population Reports*, "Characteristics of the Population below the Poverty Level: 1977," series P-60, no. 119 (March 1979), Table 38.

14. Robert S. Weiss, *Going It Alone* (New York: Basic Books, 1979).

15. Ibid.

16. Taken from Panel Study of Income Dynamics computer runs by Susan Bartlett.

17. *Current Population Reports*, series P-23, no. 75 (Nov. 1978), Table 5.

18. Taken from Panel Study of Income Dynamics computer runs by Susan Bartlett.

19. Susan Anderson-Khleif, "Income Packaging and Lifestyle in Welfare Families," *Family Policy Note* no. 7 (Cambridge, Mass.: MIT-Harvard Joint Center for Urban Studies, 1978); unpublished analyses of 1979 survey data from three cities by Richard Coleman.

20. *Current Population Reports*, series P-23, no. 75, Table 6.

21. Ibid.

22. *Social Security Bulletin Annual Statistical Supplement* (1976), Table 3.

23. Ethel P. Shanas, D. Wedderburn, H. Friis, and J. Stehouver, *Old People in Three Industrial Societies* (New York: Atherton Press, 1968).

24. *Current Population Reports,* "School Enrollment: October 1968 and 1967," series P-20, no. 190 (October 1969) and "School Enrollment—Social and Economic Characteristics of Students: October 1978," series P-20, no. 346 (October 1979).

25. Mary Jo Bane, Laura Lein, Lydia O'Donnell, C. Ann Steuve, and Barbara Welles, "Child Care in the United States," *Family Policy Note* no. 11 (Cambridge, Mass.: MIT-Harvard Joint Center for Urban Studies, 1979).

26. Fertility data are primarily reported by the National Center for Health Statistics, labor force data by the Bureau of Labor Statistics, household data by the Bureau of the Census, and education data by the National Center for Education Statistics.

Appendix A

RELATED PUBLICATIONS

Joint Center Working Papers

8. LEE RAINWATER, "Public Responses to Low Income Policies: FAP and Welfare," 1972.
9. ———, "An Exploratory Study of a Social Psychological Metric for Magnitudes of Poverty," 1972.
10. ———, "Poverty, Living Standards and Family Well-being," 1972.
15. ———, "Work, Well-being and Family Life," 1972.
20. RICHARD P. COLEMAN, "Seven Levels of Housing: An Exploration in Public Imagery," 1973.
40. BENNETT HARRISON AND MARTIN REIN, "Some Microeconomic Relationships between Work and Welfare," 1976.
43. MARTIN REIN AND FRANCINE F. RABINOVITZ, "Implementation: A Theoretical Perspective," March 1977.
47. ——— AND LEE RAINWATER, "Patterns of Welfare Use," 1977.
48. RICHARD P. COLEMAN, "Husbands, Wives, and Other Earners: Notes on the Family Income Assembly Line," 1978.
50. BENNETT HARRISON, "Labor Market Structure and the Relationship between Work and Welfare," 1978.
52. MARY JO BANE, "Family Policy in the United States: Toward a Description and Evaluation," 1978.
    JOHN R. PITKIN AND GEORGE MASNICK, "Projecting Housing Consumption in the U.S. by the Cohort Method: 1980–2000," forthcoming.

Joint Center Family Policy Notes

1. MARTIN REIN, "Notes for the Study of Tacit Family Policy," 1977.
2. LEE RAINWATER, "Family, Unions, and Youth Unemployment," 1977.
3. MARTIN REIN, "The Family and Selective Economic Growth," 1977.
4. MARTIN REIN AND LEE RAINWATER, "The Welfare Class and Welfare Reform," 1977.
5. LEE RAINWATER, "Observations on Family Policy in Europe and America," 1977.

6. ———, "Welfare and Working Mothers," 1977.
7. SUSAN ANDERSON-KHLEIF, "Income Packaging and Lifestyle in Welfare Families," 1978.
8. LEE RAINWATER, "Precious Opportunity: The Tax Cuts and Family Needs," 1978.
9. ———, "Women's Employment Preferences and Participation in the CEC Countries," 1978.
10. MARY JO BANE, "The American Divorce Rate: What Does it Mean? What Should We Worry About?" 1978.
11. ———, LAURA LEIN, LYDIA O'DONNELL, C. ANN STUEVE, AND BARBARA WELLES, "Child Care in the United States," 1979.
12. LEE RAINWATER, "Mothers' Contribution to the Family Money Economy in Europe and America," 1979.
13. MARY JO BANE, "Government and Families: Partners or Antagonists," 1979.
14. LEE RAINWATER, "Stigma in Income-Tested Programs," 1980.
15. MARTIN REIN AND LEE RAINWATER, "The Future of the Welfare State," 1980.
16. LEE RAINWATER, MARTIN REIN, AND JOSEPH SCHWARTZ, "Income Claims Systems in Three Countries: A Stratification Perspective," 1980.
17. GEORGE PENICK, "An Exploration of Federal Government Programs and Policies for Families." 1980.

Books

MARY JO BANE, *Here to Stay: American Families in the Twentieth Century* (Basic Books, 1976).
RICHARD P. COLEMAN AND LEE RAINWATER, WITH KENT A. MCCLELLAND, *Social Standing in America: New Dimensions of Class* (Basic Books, 1978).
LEE RAINWATER, *What Money Buys: Inequality and the Social Meanings of Income* (Basic Books, 1974).
LEE RAINWATER, ED., *Social Problems and Public Policy: Inequality and Justice* (Aldine, 1974).
MARTIN REIN, *Social Policy: Issues of Choice and Change* (Random House, 1970).
———, *Social Science and Public Policy* (Viking-Penguin, 1976).
ARTHUR P. SOLOMON, ED., *The Prospective City: Economic, Population, Energy and Environmental Developments Shaping Our Cities and Suburbs* (The MIT Press, 1980).

Articles

MARY JO BANE, LAURA LEIN, LYDIA O'DONNELL, ANN STEUVE, AND BARBARA WELLES, "Child Care in the United States," *Monthly Labor Review*, October 1979.

———— AND ROBERT WEISS, "Alone Together: The World of Single-Parent Families," *American Demographics* (May 1980).

————, "Marital Disruption and the Lives of Children," *Journal of Social Issues* 32:1 (1976). Revised version in *Divorce and Separation*, George Levinger and Oliver Moles, eds. (Basic Books, 1978).

————, "Children, Divorce and Welfare," *Wilson Quarterly* (Winter 1977).

————, "Who Cares about Day Care?" *Working Papers* (Spring 1974).

GEORGE MASNICK AND JOHN R. PITKIN, "Analysis and Projection of Housing Consumption by Birth Cohorts: 1960–2000," a research report prepared by the Joint Center for Urban Studies of MIT and Harvard University for U.S. Department of Housing and Urban Development Grant #H-2842RG.

————, DOWELL MYERS, JOHN R. PITKIN, AND BARBARA WIGET, "A Life Course Perspective on the Downturn in U.S. Fertility," *Working Paper* no. 106 (Harvard Center for Population Studies, 1978).

———— AND JOSEPH MCFALLS, "Those Perplexing U.S. Fertility Swings: A New Perspective on a 20th Century Puzzle," *Population Reference Bureau Report* (November 1978).

———— AND JOSEPH MCFALLS, "A New Perspective on the 20th Century Fertility Swing," *Journal of Family History* 1 (1977).

LEE RAINWATER, "Notes on U.S. Family Policy," *Social Policy* (March–April 1978).

LEE RAINWATER, "Mothers' Contribution to the Family Economy in Europe and the United States," *Journal of Family History* (Summer 1979).

————, "Equity, Income Inequality and the Steady States," in *The Sustainable Society*, Dennis C. Pirages, ed. (Praeger, 1977).

MARTIN REIN, "The Labor Utilization Framework," in *Counting the Labor Force* (National Commission on Employment and Unemployment Statistics, 1979).

————, "Services In-Kind," paper prepared for the Conference on Universal vs. Income-Tested Transfer Programs sponsored by the Institute of Research on Poverty (University of Wisconsin, 1979).

———— AND LEE RAINWATER, "Patterns of Welfare Use," *Social Science Review* (December 1978).

————, "How Large is the Welfare Class?" *Challenge* 20:4 (1977).

————, "Equality and Social Policy," *Social Service Review* (December 1977).

———— AND SHELDON WHITE, "Practice Worries and Coordination of Social Services," prepared for OECD (May 1977).

————, "A Model for Income Support Programs: Experience with Public Assistance and Implications for a Direct Cash Assistance Program," prepared for U.S. Department of Housing and Urban Development (Abt Associates, 1975).

———— AND PETER MARRIS, "Equality, Inflation and Wage Control," *Challenge* 18:1 (1975).

———— AND S. M. MILLER, "The Possibilities of Income Transformation," *Social Policy* (June 1975).

———— AND BERNARD FRIEDEN, "Cash Assistance in Public Programs," in "Analysis of Selected Census and Welfare Program Data to Determine Housing Market Characteristics, and Administrative Welfare Policies to a Direct Housing Assistance Program," final report submitted to U.S. Department of Housing and Urban Development (1974).

Appendix B

TABLES RELATING TO CHAPTERS 1 AND 2

Procedure for Table B.1

Estimates and projections of the number of households were calculated by John Pitkin using the methods described in John Pitkin and George Masnick, "Analysis and Projection of Housing Consumption by Birth Cohorts: 1960–2000," a research report prepared by the MIT-Harvard Joint Center for Urban Studies for U.S. Department of Housing and Urban Development Grant #H-2842RG. For the purposes of estimating labor force participation rates, households were broken down into those with children and those without, and those with a head 65 years of age or over and those with a head under age 65. Estimates of work status were then calculated as follows in the tables below. The appropriate labor force participation rates were then applied to the distribution of households to estimate the number of households in each category, as shown in Table B.10.

1960: Labor force participation rates for 1960 were taken from Tables 4 and 8 of U.S. Bureau of the Census, *Census of the Population: 1960*, "Employment Status and Work Experience," Subject Report 6A (Washington, D.C., GPO, 1963):

Household Type	Percentages
Male Household Heads	
Married Spouse Present	88.6
Other Marital Statuses	69.0
Female Wives of Household Heads	30.7
Female Heads	
With Children	58.6
Without Children	45.8

1975: Labor force participation rates were estimated from rates by marital status reported in the *Special Labor Force Reports*. For never-married men and women, the labor force participation rates of those over 25 were used as estimates for the rates of household heads:

Household Type	Percentages
Male Family Heads	
Husband/Wife Families	82.9
Male Family Heads, Other	74.8
Wives of Family Heads	44.6
Female Family Heads	
With Children	62.4
Without Children	42.0
Divorced, Separated, Widowed Males	65.2
Never-Married Males over 25	73.3
Divorced, Separated, Never-Married (25+) Females	
Without Children	48.3

1990: Projections of labor force participation rates came from three sources: Urban Institute projections for women 20–54 by marital status and presence of children; Bureau of Labor Statistics projections for women 55–64; and 1978 rates for male family heads and for men and women 65+ [a]. Weighted averages were calculated:

Household Type	Percentages
Married Women without Children	60.0
Married Women with Children	64.9
Never- and Other Ever-Married Women without Children	71.4
Other Ever-Married with Children	70.8
Males under 65 in Husband/Wife Families	90.0
Males over 65 in Husband/Wife Families	21.0
Male Household Heads under 65	90.0
Male Household Heads 65+	15.0

[a] Ralph Smith, *Women in The Labor Force* (Washington, D.C.: The Urban Institute, 1979), Tables 3 and 4. P. Flain and H. Fullerton, Jr., "Labor Force Projections to 1990: Three Possible Paths," *Monthly Labor Review* 101:12 (1978), 25–35.

Table B.1. Back-Up Table for Figure 1.2: Labor Force Participation of Households by Rate and Number, 1960, 1975, and 1990

	Year					
	1960		1975		1990	
Household Type	LFP[a] Rate (%)	Households (1,000,000)	LFP Rate (%)	Households (1,000,000)	LFP Rate (%)	Households (1,000,000)
Female Heads with Children	59	1.7	62	4.2	71	6.6
LF Participants		1.0		2.6		4.7
Not Participants		0.7		1.6		1.9
Female Heads without Children	46	7.3	50	13.7	41	20.4
LF Participants		3.4		6.8		8.4
Not Participants		3.9		6.9		12.0
Male Heads	70	4.3	70	8.3	76	14.8
LF Participants		3.0		5.8		12.1
Not Participants		1.3		2.5		3.9
Husband/Wife Families		39.6		51.0		50.9
Husband	79		73		73	
Wife	31		45		57	
One Worker		22.9		19.4		13.2
Two Workers		12.2		22.9		28.9
No Worker		4.5		8.7		8.8
Total		57.3		77.2		92.7

[a] Labor force participation rate.

Tables B.2. Back-Up Tables for Figures 2.1 and 2.2: Household Population of the United States by Age, Sex, and Relationship to Head, 1940–1970

B.2.a. Household Population, 1940

Age Group	Male			Female			
	Head	Child	Other	Head	Wife	Child	Other
0–4	—	4,767,585	571,542	—	—	4,605,714	566,996
5–9	—	4,941,817	446,818	—	—	4,794,483	446,044
10–14	529	5,444,134	447,793	293	1,887	5,294,865	451,119
15–19	61,408	5,378,398	595,179	15,070	463,904	4,840,193	729,145
20–24	1,198,003	3,320,949	909,493	97,551	2,373,323	2,338,303	924,683
25–29	2,953,187	1,465,525	810,778	189,746	3,579,904	1,088,794	669,123
30–34	3,585,828	701,429	599,680	280,711	3,701,206	624,228	465,444
35–39	3,682,474	384,166	502,845	399,437	3,553,050	379,927	373,990
40–44	3,603,782	212,426	427,867	479,142	3,240,206	233,559	326,587
45–49	3,541,466	114,805	385,019	551,766	2,933,750	142,869	330,589
50–54	3,174,344	59,843	364,074	591,888	2,373,817	81,611	375,530
55–59	2,551,137	25,695	311,722	578,953	1,748,436	38,103	397,567
60–64	2,002,722	9,277	284,321	574,967	1,228,208	15,936	450,464
65–69	1,539,726	—	278,441	575,456	789,825	—	492,945
70–74	978,681	—	235,855	447,413	386,127	—	420,884
75+	806,431	—	362,170	486,555	196,859	—	649,002

SOURCE: U.S. Bureau of the Census, *Sixteenth Census of the United States: 1940*, "Characteristics by Age," vol. 4:1, U.S. Summary (Washington, D.C.: GPO, 1943), Table 11.

B.2.b. Household Population, 1950

Age Group	Male			Female			
	Head	Child	Other	Head	Wife	Child	Other
0–4	—	7,354,105	857,555	—	—	7,057,260	847,380
5–9	—	6,141,505	522,555	—	—	5,926,165	524,530
10–14	5,955	5,169,665	428,045	1,215	2,170	5,014,680	304,100
15–19	101,360	4,271,675	488,255	26,000	579,115	3,834,690	587,345
20–24	1,742,360	2,304,265	770,305	136,775	3,070,440	1,626,285	720,585
25–29	3,825,675	1,048,620	662,730	233,130	4,520,480	858,965	509,970
30–34	4,313,105	542,435	463,040	308,235	4,565,575	541,410	355,095
35–39	4,471,500	346,035	397,740	422,885	4,450,360	385,510	327,395
40–44	4,204,100	219,375	346,130	515,245	3,913,700	265,135	313,715
45–49	3,801,925	123,830	318,155	594,825	3,347,980	160,340	332,760
50–54	3,471,540	62,300	301,870	668,705	2,854,935	95,295	397,890
55–59	3,060,805	27,015	289,500	699,005	2,294,275	48,580	453,235
60–64	2,511,150	10,400	297,165	711,300	1,653,690	21,565	538,075
65–69	1,961,610	4,780	303,440	754,420	1,133,425	9,585	607,870
70–74	1,253,055	—	261,145	601,785	573,050	—	543,385
75+	1,138,760	—	454,235	717,990	316,680	—	919,850

SOURCE: U.S. Bureau of the Census, *U.S. Census of the Population: 1950,* "Characteristics of the Population," vol. 1, Detailed Characteristics (1953), Table 107.

B.2.c. Household Population, 1960

Age Group	Male			Female			
	Head	Child	Other	Head	Wife	Child	Other
0–4	—	9,575,710	737,670	—	—	9,238,706	721,121
5–9	—	8,981,339	466,748	—	—	8,676,769	461,797
10–14	1,799	8,077,280	406,991	793	5,253	7,796,963	400,726
15–19	179,813	5,381,074	481,418	57,702	729,961	4,873,581	550,281
20–24	2,187,431	1,707,226	552,091	271,207	3,330,247	1,169,369	474,005
25–29	4,004,104	719,976	364,403	348,678	4,378,166	494,185	250,218
30–34	4,960,014	427,824	270,776	454,495	5,050,974	354,178	190,858
35–39	5,384,635	302,278	241,511	572,437	5,307,225	295,033	181,999
40–44	5,094,890	203,354	221,015	654,823	4,781,738	221,259	195,133
45–49	4,877,630	145,256	230,643	760,473	4,306,436	170,381	242,779
50–54	4,316,362	97,069	236,412	846,754	3,566,823	125,898	314,066
55–59	3,763,706	56,831	255,729	948,001	2,884,832	81,222	415,491
60–64	3,039,515	16,363	229,296	1,006,621	2,131,920	28,864	480,498
65–69	2,553,505	6,046	236,989	1,084,976	1,569,507	12,969	554,761
70–74	1,823,621	2,856	235,240	962,032	890,712	6,039	572,398
75+	1,686,035	44	440,769	1,181,873	541,130	102	1,065,249

SOURCE: U.S. Bureau of the Census, *U.S. Census of the Population: 1960*, "Characteristics of the Population," vol. 1:1, Detailed Characteristics (1964), Table 181.

B.2.d. Household Population, 1970

Age Group	Male			Female			
	Head	Child	Other	Head	Wife	Child	Other
0–4	—	8,064,919	644,156	—	—	7,745,298	632,121
5–9	—	9,734,581	435,088	—	—	9,371,676	442,481
10–14	16,476	10,117,298	403,165	5,110	11,464	9,739,611	422,526
15–19	323,423	7,955,194	533,257	124,099	764,434	7,350,212	609,558
20–24	3,408,309	2,447,338	693,099	768,904	4,381,234	2,027,880	703,925
25–29	5,275,175	762,287	332,113	772,845	5,177,543	540,910	228,663
30–34	4,952,581	347,995	178,176	683,189	4,689,929	283,612	157,618
35–39	4,942,447	247,582	147,481	701,127	4,617,380	216,263	136,520
40–44	5,364,451	210,528	160,518	829,637	4,925,308	194,465	161,049
45–49	5,422,548	159,520	163,777	941,045	4,898,984	167,766	193,855
50–54	4,983,532	106,748	169,341	1,046,413	4,260,008	126,887	247,438
55–59	4,467,809	60,337	171,587	1,204,882	3,557,526	84,955	316,247
60–64	3,762,881	27,680	176,867	1,368,884	2,723,208	46,219	397,638
65–69	2,859,531	12,675	170,141	1,451,931	1,873,858	22,032	448,002
70–74	2,085,184	7,931	156,560	1,395,367	1,142,148	11,158	471,803
75+	2,383,428	27,813	370,187	2,087,513	846,130	28,690	1,146,657

SOURCE: U.S. Bureau of the Census, *U.S. Census of the Population: 1970*, "Characteristics of the Population," vol. 1:1, sec. 2, U.S. Summary (1973), Table 204.

Table B.3. Back-Up Table for Figure 2.3: Husband/Wife Couples and Unrelated Individuals, 1947–1979

Year	*Ratio of Married Couple Household Heads to Unrelated Individual Household Heads*	*Ratio of All Married Couples to All Unrelated Individuals in Population*	*Ratio of Female to Male Unrelated Individuals in Population*
1947	7.39	3.95	1.20
1948	8.17	4.14	1.16
1949	8.11	4.17	1.08
1950	7.23	3.95	1.17
1951	6.65	3.80	1.27
1952	6.63	3.95	1.30
1953	6.09	3.73	1.29
1954	6.02	3.83	1.38
1955	5.90	3.80	1.36
1956	5.87	3.82	1.36
1957	5.88	3.93	1.42
1958	5.38	3.70	1.45
1959	5.15	3.57	1.44
1960	4.97	3.62	1.49
1961	4.85	3.61	1.60
1962	4.75	3.57	1.52
1963	4.87	3.69	1.58
1964	4.71	3.69	1.60
1965	4.34	3.44	1.62
1966	4.22	3.42	1.69
1967	4.21	3.42	1.70
1968	4.02	3.29	1.71
1969	3.84	3.16	1.67
1970	3.74	3.03	1.63
1971	3.54	2.88	1.57
1972	3.38	2.80	1.52
1973	3.31	2.74	1.50
1974	3.13	2.55	1.41
1975	3.02	2.49	1.39
1976	2.81	2.33	1.41
1977	2.69	2.21	1.36
1978	2.48	2.05	1.30
1979	2.40	1.94	1.30

SOURCE: *Current Population Reports*, "Households and Families by Type: March 1979 (Advance Report)," series P-20, no. 345 (October 1979), Table 3.

Table B.4. **Back-Up Table for Figure 2.4: Percentage of Population Never Married, 1890–1990**

Year	Men's Ages				Women's Ages			
	15–19	*20–24*	*25–29*	*30–34*	*15–19*	*20–24*	*25–29*	*30–34*
1890	99.45	80.69	45.98	26.50	90.30	51.79	25.38	15.16
1900	98.82	77.58	45.76	27.60	88.68	51.57	27.54	16.63
1910	98.25	74.93	42.79	26.03	87.86	48.33	24.94	16.14
1920	97.73	70.70	39.44	24.11	86.98	45.56	23.05	14.93
1930	98.04	70.82	36.74	21.17	86.85	44.40	21.71	13.23
1940	98.27	72.19	36.03	20.71	88.15	47.17	22.81	14.73
1950	96.68	59.03	23.79	13.20	82.92	32.30	13.27	9.26
1960	96.09	53.14	20.85	11.90	83.91	28.40	10.51	6.92
1970	95.86	55.50	19.61	10.73	88.12	36.28	12.16	7.43
1975	97.30	63.10	26.20	13.00	89.20	44.00	16.00	8.20
1978	97.90[a]	65.80	27.80	12.80	91.93[a]	47.60	18.00	8.40
1980	98.00	70.00	27.00	13.80	90.00	51.00	20.00	9.80
1985	98.00	80.00	34.10	14.40	90.00	54.60	25.50	12.10
1990	98.00	85.00	46.10	18.70	90.00	54.60	28.40	15.20

Sources: 1890–1970: U.S. Bureau of the Census, *Historical Statistics of the United States: Colonial Times to 1970*, part 1 (Washington, D.C.: GPO, 1975), pp. 20–21. 1975: Estimated by adjusting June 1975 CPS data to represent total U.S. population. 1978: Refers to CPS population base, *Current Population Reports*, series P-20, no. 338 (May 1979), Table 1. 1980–1990: Joint Center for Urban Studies projections.

[a] Values for 14–19 age group.

Table B.5.   Back-Up Table for Table 2.4: Interpolated Cohort Rates: Percentage Never-Married Females, 1901–1960

Cohort	Age									
	20	21	22	23	24	25	26	27	28	29
1901	60.05	52.58	44.93	38.22	32.70	28.58	24.53	21.04	18.94	15.60
1902	60.10	52.62	44.94	38.20	32.64	28.51	24.42	21.92	18.80	15.81
1903	60.15	52.66	44.95	38.18	32.58	28.44	24.31	20.80	18.93	16.02
1904	60.20	52.70	44.96	38.16	32.52	28.37	24.20	21.92	19.02	16.23
1905	60.25	52.74	44.97	38.14	32.46	28.30	24.29	21.04	19.19	16.44
1906	60.30	52.78	44.98	38.12	32.40	28.33	24.38	21.16	19.32	16.55
1907	60.35	52.82	44.99	38.10	32.45	28.36	24.47	21.28	19.45	16.86
1908	60.40	52.86	45.00	38.16	32.50	28.39	24.56	21.40	19.58	17.07
1909	60.45	52.90	45.12	38.22	32.55	28.42	24.65	21.52	19.71	17.28
1910	60.50	53.05	45.24	38.28	32.60	28.45	24.74	21.64	19.84	17.49
1911	60.73	53.20	45.36	38.34	32.65	28.48	24.83	21.76	19.97	17.70
1912	60.96	53.35	45.48	38.40	32.70	28.51	24.92	21.88	20.10	16.97
1913	61.19	53.50	45.60	38.46	32.75	28.54	25.01	22.00	19.25	16.24
1914	61.42	53.65	45.72	38.52	32.80	28.57	25.10	21.07	18.40	15.51
1915	61.65	53.80	45.84	38.58	32.85	28.60	24.09	20.14	17.55	14.78
1916	61.88	53.95	45.96	38.64	32.90	27.39	23.08	19.21	16.70	14.05
1917	62.11	54.10	46.08	38.70	31.59	26.18	22.07	18.28	15.85	13.32
1918	62.34	54.25	46.20	37.22	30.28	24.97	21.06	17.35	15.00	12.59
1919	62.57	54.40	44.59	35.74	28.97	23.76	20.05	16.42	14.15	11.86
1920	62.82	52.83	42.98	34.26	27.66	22.55	19.04	15.49	13.30	11.13

Table B.5. (continued)

Cohort	Age									
	20	21	22	23	24	25	26	27	28	29
1921	61.52	51.26	41.37	32.78	26.35	21.34	18.03	14.56	12.45	10.40
1922	60.24	49.69	39.76	31.30	25.04	20.13	17.02	16.63	11.60	10.23
1923	58.96	48.12	38.15	29.82	23.73	18.92	16.01	12.70	11.37	10.06
1924	57.68	46.55	36.54	28.34	22.42	17.71	15.00	12.42	11.14	9.89
1925	56.40	44.98	34.93	26.86	21.11	16.50	14.65	12.14	10.91	9.72
1926	55.12	43.41	33.32	25.38	19.80	16.16	14.30	11.86	10.68	9.55
1927	53.84	41.84	31.71	23.90	19.38	15.82	13.95	11.58	10.45	9.38
1928	52.56	40.27	30.10	23.45	18.96	15.48	13.60	11.30	10.22	9.21
1929	51.28	38.70	29.67	23.00	18.54	15.14	13.25	11.02	9.99	9.04
1930	50.00	38.34	29.24	22.55	18.12	14.80	12.90	10.74	9.76	8.87
1931	49.58	37.98	28.81	22.10	17.70	14.46	12.55	10.46	9.53	8.70
1932	49.16	37.62	28.38	21.65	17.28	14.12	12.20	10.18	9.30	8.76
1933	48.74	37.26	27.95	21.20	16.86	13.78	11.85	9.90	9.40	8.82
1934	48.32	36.90	27.52	20.75	16.44	13.44	11.50	10.05	9.50	8.88
1935	47.90	36.54	27.09	20.30	16.02	13.10	11.67	10.20	9.60	8.94
1936	47.48	36.18	26.66	19.85	15.60	13.41	11.84	10.35	9.70	9.00
1937	47.06	35.82	26.23	19.40	16.03	13.72	12.01	10.50	9.80	9.06
1938	46.64	35.46	25.80	19.92	16.46	14.03	12.18	10.65	9.90	9.12
1939	46.22	35.10	26.44	20.44	16.89	14.34	12.35	10.80	10.00	9.18
1940	45.80	36.03	27.08	20.96	17.32	14.65	12.52	10.95	10.10	9.24

Table B.5. (continued)

Cohort	Age									
	20	21	22	23	24	25	26	27	28	29
1941	46.89	36.96	27.72	21.48	17.75	14.96	12.69	11.10	10.20	9.30
1942	47.98	37.89	28.36	22.00	18.18	15.27	12.86	11.25	10.30	(9.97)
1943	49.07	38.82	29.00	22.52	18.61	15.58	13.03	11.40	(11.02)	(10.64)
1944	50.16	39.75	29.64	23.04	19.04	15.89	13.20	(12.26)	(11.74)	(11.31)
1945	51.25	40.68	30.28	23.56	19.47	16.20	(14.23)	(13.12)	(12.46)	(11.98)
1946	52.34	41.61	30.92	24.08	19.90	(17.43)	(15.26)	(13.98)	(13.18)	(12.65)
1947	53.43	42.54	31.56	24.60	(21.41)	(18.66)	(16.29)	(14.84)	(13.90)	(13.32)
1948	54.52	43.47	32.20	(26.44)	(22.92)	(19.89)	(17.32)	(15.70)	(14.62)	(13.99)
1949	55.61	44.40	(34.08)	(28.28)	(24.43)	(21.12)	(18.35)	(16.56)	(15.34)	(14.66)
1950	56.70	(45.96)	(35.96)	(30.12)	(25.94)	(22.35)	(19.38)	(17.42)	(16.06)	(15.33)
1951	(57.83)	(47.52)	(37.84)	(31.96)	(27.45)	(23.58)	(20.41)	(18.28)	(16.78)	(16.00)
1952	(58.96)	(49.08)	(39.72)	(33.80)	(28.96)	(24.81)	(21.44)	(19.14)	(17.50)	
1953	(60.09)	(50.64)	(41.60)	(35.64)	(30.47)	(26.04)	(22.47)	(20.00)		
1954	(61.22)	(52.20)	(43.48)	(37.48)	(31.98)	(27.27)	(23.50)			
1955	(62.35)	(53.76)	(45.36)	(39.32)	(33.49)	(28.50)				
1956	(63.48)	(55.32)	(47.24)	(41.16)	(35.00)					
1957	(64.61)	(56.88)	(49.12)	(43.00)						
1958	(65.74)	(58.44)	(51.00)							
1959	(66.87)	(60.00)								
1960	(68.00)									

SOURCE: U.S. Bureau of the Census, *Historical Statistics of the United States: Colonial Times to 1970*, part 1 (Washington. D.C.: GPO, 1975), pp. 20–21.

Table B.6. Back-Up Table for Figure 2.5: Divorced Individuals as a Proportion of Those Ever Married, 1866–1875 to 1946–1955 Birth Cohorts

Cohort of Birth	Men's Ages					Women's Ages				
	15–24	25–34	35–44	45–54	55–64	15–24	25–34	35–44	45–54	55–64
1866–1875	.0024	.0047	.0105	.0113	.0170	.0044	.0079	.0101	.0111	.0125
1876–1885	.0041	.0067	.0103	.0185	.0203	.0070	.0100	.0125	.0175	.0172
1886–1895	.0058	.0087	.0182	.0223	.0290	.0084	.0119	.0209	.0243	.0264
1896–1905	.0077	.0167	.0220	.0323	.0333	.0108	.0226	.0303	.0377	.0395
1906–1915	.0139	.0160	.0281	.0331	.0402	.0120	.0259	.0390	.0458	.0537
1916–1925	.0110	.0235	.0282	.0410	****	.0168	.0310	.0407	.0585	****
1926–1935	.0227	.0237	.0391	****	****	.0232	.0317	.0578	****	****
1936–1945	.0214	.0368	****	****	****	.0244	.0513	****	****	****
1946–1955	.0321	****	****	****	****	.0378	****	****	****	****

SOURCE: U.S. Bureau of the Census, *Historical Statistics of the United States: Colonial Times to 1970*, part 1 (Washington, D.C.: GPO, 1975), pp. 20–21.

Table B.7. Percentage Distribution of Marital Status for U.S., 1975 Estimates and 1990 Projected Values

Ages	Never Married				Married Spouse Present				Divorced/Separated Spouse Absent				Widowed			
	1975	1980	1985	1990	1975	1980	1985	1990	1975	1980	1985	1990	1975	1980	1985	1990
Women																
15–19	89.2	90.0	90.0	90.0	9.8	8.8	8.7	8.6	0.9	1.2	1.3	1.4	0.0	0.0	0.0	0.0
20–24	44.0	51.0	54.6	54.6	50.0	42.0	38.2	37.8	5.8	6.9	7.1	7.5	0.2	0.1	0.1	0.1
25–29	16.0	20.0	25.5	28.4	71.4	64.1	58.1	54.8	12.0	15.4	16.0	16.4	0.5	0.4	0.4	0.4
30–34	8.2	9.8	12.1	15.2	77.8	72.0	68.2	64.6	13.1	17.4	18.9	19.4	0.9	0.8	0.8	0.8
35–39	5.4	6.2	7.2	8.5	79.6	74.4	71.7	69.4	13.3	17.8	19.6	20.6	1.7	1.6	1.6	1.5
40–44	3.6	5.4	6.1	6.8	85.0	80.4	78.5	77.0	9.0	11.9	13.2	13.9	2.4	2.3	2.2	2.2
45–49	4.4	3.9	5.5	6.1	77.8	73.9	70.9	69.3	12.1	16.5	18.0	19.1	5.7	5.7	5.6	5.6
50–54	4.7	5.1	4.6	6.1	76.8	73.2	72.2	70.2	9.3	12.5	14.0	14.7	9.2	9.1	9.2	9.0
55–59	5.3	4.8	5.2	4.0	70.9	68.2	66.6	66.1	8.6	11.6	12.9	13.8	15.3	15.3	15.3	15.4
60–64	6.5	6.0	5.6	6.0	62.3	60.4	59.7	58.5	6.4	8.6	9.6	10.3	24.8	25.0	25.1	25.0
65–69	6.6	7.0	6.5	6.2	51.4	48.9	48.2	47.7	6.6	8.9	9.9	10.6	35.4	35.2	35.4	35.5
70–74	7.9	6.9	7.2	6.8	39.8	38.6	37.7	37.4	4.8	6.5	7.3	7.8	47.5	48.0	47.8	48.0
75–79	8.2	7.9	6.9	7.2	24.8	23.4	23.0	22.5	4.3	5.8	6.5	7.0	62.7	62.9	63.5	63.3
80–84	8.1	8.2	7.9	6.9	15.1	13.6	13.1	12.8	4.1	5.6	6.2	6.7	72.7	72.6	72.9	73.6
85+	8.1	8.1	8.2	7.9	9.5	8.0	7.4	7.0	4.2	5.6	6.2	6.7	78.3	78.3	78.2	78.5

Table B.7. (continued)

Ages	Never Married				Married Spouse Present				Divorced/Separated Spouse Absent				Widowed			
	1975	1980	1985	1990	1975	1980	1985	1990	1975	1980	1985	1990	1975	1980	1985	1990
Men																
15–19	97.3	98.0	98.0	98.0	2.5	1.8	1.8	1.7	0.2	0.2	0.2	0.3	0.0	0.0	0.0	0.0
20–24	63.1	70.0	80.0	85.0	32.9	25.5	16.4	12.0	4.0	4.5	3.6	3.0	0.0	0.0	0.0	0.0
25–29	26.2	27.0	34.1	46.1	65.0	60.8	52.9	42.0	8.8	12.2	13.0	11.9	0.0	0.0	0.0	0.0
30–34	13.0	13.8	14.4	18.7	77.8	73.5	70.9	65.6	8.9	12.4	14.5	15.5	0.3	0.2	0.2	0.2
35–39	9.4	8.7	9.2	9.4	82.6	80.2	77.9	76.1	7.7	10.9	12.8	14.3	0.2	0.2	0.2	0.2
40–44	5.6	8.3	7.7	8.0	86.6	81.2	79.9	78.2	7.5	10.1	12.0	13.4	0.4	0.3	0.4	0.3
45–49	6.0	5.4	7.7	7.2	85.9	83.4	79.6	78.6	7.3	10.2	11.8	13.3	0.9	0.9	0.9	0.9
50–54	5.2	5.9	5.4	7.4	85.6	82.1	80.7	77.5	7.3	10.1	12.0	13.1	1.9	1.9	1.9	1.9
55–59	6.3	5.5	6.2	5.7	84.8	83.1	81.0	80.2	6.0	8.5	10.0	11.2	2.9	2.9	2.9	2.9
60–64	4.5	6.3	5.7	6.2	84.8	80.8	79.8	78.1	6.2	8.5	10.1	11.3	4.4	4.3	4.4	4.4
65–69	6.1	5.1	6.6	6.1	80.7	79.3	76.6	76.0	5.5	7.8	9.1	10.3	7.7	7.8	7.7	7.7
70–74	5.0	6.1	5.1	6.6	77.4	74.6	74.1	72.0	5.0	6.9	8.2	9.0	12.6	12.5	12.6	12.4
75–79	5.9	5.0	6.1	5.1	67.3	66.6	65.0	64.9	3.5	5.0	5.8	6.6	23.2	23.4	23.2	23.4
80–84	5.8	5.9	5.0	6.1	56.2	54.8	54.5	53.1	3.5	4.9	5.8	6.4	34.5	34.4	34.8	34.4
85+	5.7	5.8	5.9	5.0	44.8	43.4	42.5	42.3	3.4	4.8	5.6	6.4	46.0	46.0	45.9	46.0

SOURCE: John Pitkin and George Masnick, "Analysis and Projection of Housing Consumption by Birth Cohorts: 1960–2000," a research report prepared by the MIT-Harvard Joint Center for Urban Studies for U.S. Department of Housing and Urban Development Grant #H-2842RG.

Table B.8.   Back-Up Table for Figure 2.7: Annual Number of Births, 1929–1979 (thousands)

Pre-WWII Fertility		Baby Boom Fertility		Recent Fertility Downswing	
Year	*Births*	*Year*	*Births*	*Year*	*Births*
1929	2,582	1946	3,411	1963	4,185
1930	2,618	1947	3,817	1964	4,119
1931	2,506	1948	3,637	1965	3,940
1932	2,440	1949	3,649	1966	3,716
1933	2,307	1950	3,632	1967	3,608
1934	2,396	1951	3,823	1968	3,520
1935	2,377	1952	3,913	1969	3,567
1936	2,355	1953	3,965	1970	3,660
1937	2,413	1954	4,078	1971	3,705
1938	2,496	1955	4,104	1972	3,407
1939	2,466	1956	4,218	1973	3,191
1940	2,559	1957	4,312	1974	3,160
1941	2,703	1958	4,313	1975	3,144
1942	2,989	1959	4,298	1976	3,165
1943	3,104	1960	4,279	1977	3,326
1944	2,939	1961	4,350	1978	3,329
1945	2,858	1962	4,259	1979	3,473

SOURCE: National Center for Health Statistics, *Vital Statistics of the United States* and *Monthly Vital Statistics Report* (various issues).

Table B.9.   Back-Up Table for Figures 2.8, 2.9, and 2.10: Parity Distribution by Cohort

Cohorts and Parity Distribution	Age														
	20	21	22	23	24	25	26	27	28	29	30	31	32	33	34
1901															
0–1[a]	94.43	90.26	85.21	79.80	74.35	69.46	65.13	61.36	58.07	55.22	52.63	50.54	48.81	47.48	46.29
2–3	5.41	9.27	13.75	18.17	22.06	25.00	27.19	28.79	30.05	31.09	31.93	32.53	32.92	33.11	33.23
4+	0.16	0.47	1.04	2.03	3.59	5.54	7.68	9.85	11.88	13.69	15.44	16.93	18.27	19.41	20.48
1906															
0–1	93.81	89.70	85.09	80.56	76.18	72.07	68.38	65.14	62.30	59.66	57.32	55.33	53.56	51.99	50.61
2–3	5.99	9.77	13.75	17.32	20.38	22.88	24.90	26.47	27.71	28.82	29.76	30.57	31.27	31.91	32.43
4+	0.20	0.53	1.16	2.12	3.44	5.05	6.72	8.39	9.99	11.52	12.91	14.10	15.17	16.10	16.96
1911															
0–1	94.30	90.80	86.86	83.00	79.09	75.52	72.16	68.97	65.84	62.97	60.18	57.59	55.08	52.62	50.51
2–3	5.52	8.76	12.20	15.28	18.06	20.31	22.28	24.10	25.86	27.48	29.06	30.55	32.02	33.39	34.43
4+	0.18	0.44	0.94	1.72	2.85	4.17	5.56	6.93	8.30	9.55	10.76	11.86	12.90	13.99	15.06
1916															
0–1	95.29	92.10	88.32	84.21	80.16	76.14	72.11	67.85	63.19	59.18	55.34	51.52	48.10	45.45	43.25
2–3	4.57	7.52	10.85	14.24	17.30	20.05	22.76	25.69	28.88	31.44	33.90	36.34	38.41	39.81	40.78
4+	0.14	0.38	0.73	1.55	2.54	3.81	5.13	6.46	7.93	9.38	10.76	12.14	13.49	14.74	15.97
1921															
0–1	94.44	90.82	86.70	81.73	77.00	72.70	66.97	60.95	55.46	50.41	45.94	42.11	38.87	36.30	34.19
2–3	5.38	8.73	12.32	16.42	19.96	22.99	27.26	31.80	35.75	39.16	41.91	43.96	45.34	46.10	46.42
4+	0.18	0.45	0.98	1.85	3.04	4.31	5.77	7.25	8.79	10.43	12.15	13.93	15.79	17.60	19.39
1926															
0–1	94.52	90.64	85.33	78.74	71.59	64.52	57.60	51.16	45.43	40.51	36.50	33.31	30.77	28.85	27.36
2–3	5.25	8.82	13.60	19.33	25.21	30.68	35.69	39.98	43.37	45.78	47.23	47.91	48.05	47.78	47.30
4+	0.23	0.54	1.07	1.93	3.20	4.80	6.71	8.86	11.20	13.71	16.27	18.78	21.18	23.37	25.34

Table B.9. (continued)

Cohorts and Parity Distribution	Age														
	20	21	22	23	24	25	26	27	28	29	30	31	32	33	34
1931															
0–1	91.01	85.13	78.15	70.34	62.31	54.62	47.51	41.26	36.20	32.17	28.99	26.56	24.74	23.34	22.24
2–3	8.64	13.98	19.96	26.26	32.26	37.50	41.79	44.99	46.90	47.74	47.87	47.47	46.87	46.18	45.52
4+	0.35	0.89	1.89	3.40	5.43	7.88	10.70	13.75	16.90	20.09	23.14	25.97	28.39	30.48	32.24
1936															
0–1	89.15	81.98	73.45	64.47	55.77	47.94	41.39	36.15	32.02	28.75	26.27	24.40	22.96	21.82	20.90
2–3	10.32	16.73	23.95	30.95	37.02	41.70	44.81	46.60	47.45	47.72	47.72	47.59	47.36	47.14	46.87
4+	0.53	1.29	2.60	4.58	7.21	10.36	13.80	17.25	20.53	23.52	26.01	28.01	29.68	31.04	32.23
1941															
0–1	88.01	80.87	72.85	64.81	57.44	51.17	45.82	41.21	37.30	33.90	31.05	28.89	27.24	26.00	25.02
2–3	11.36	17.61	24.22	30.35	35.49	39.52	42.82	45.48	47.52	49.02	50.04	50.64	51.12	51.44	51.67
4+	0.63	1.52	2.93	4.84	7.07	9.31	11.36	13.31	15.18	17.08	18.91	20.47	21.64	22.56	23.31
1942															
0–1	88.48	81.66	74.04	66.48	59.71	53.66	48.21	43.44	39.18	35.52	32.68	30.47	28.79	27.45	26.43
2–3	10.89	16.89	23.23	29.11	34.06	38.32	41.99	45.00	47.40	49.20	50.39	51.34	52.00	52.51	52.83
4+	0.63	1.45	2.73	4.41	6.23	8.02	9.80	11.56	13.42	15.28	16.93	18.19	19.21	20.04	20.74
1943															
0–1	89.00	82.58	75.50	68.66	62.23	56.13	50.63	45.61	41.15	37.59	34.76	32.62	30.73	29.35	28.27
2–3	10.41	16.08	22.03	27.49	32.46	37.01	40.92	44.22	46.89	48.80	50.30	51.44	52.32	52.91	53.31
4+	0.59	1.34	2.47	3.85	5.31	6.86	8.45	10.17	11.96	13.61	14.94	15.94	16.95	17.74	18.42
1944															
0–1	89.45	83.49	77.18	70.78	64.37	58.33	52.62	47.43	43.13	39.65	36.79	34.43	32.58	31.11	
2–3	10.00	15.29	20.66	25.94	31.08	35.75	39.92	43.45	46.17	48.33	50.06	51.44	52.42	53.13	
4+	0.59	1.34	2.16	3.28	4.55	5.92	7.46	9.12	10.70	12.02	13.15	14.13	15.00	15.76	

	20	21	22	23	24	25	26	27	28	29	30	31	32	33	34
1945															
0–1	90.00	84.64	78.91	72.69	66.53	60.45	54.67	49.74	45.65	42.13	39.12	36.69	34.70		
2–3	9.48	14.17	19.21	24.46	29.50	34.27	38.58	42.06	44.90	47.31	49.30	50.82	51.98		
4+	0.52	1.19	1.88	2.85	3.97	5.28	6.75	8.20	9.45	10.56	11.58	12.49	13.32		
1946															
0–1	90.91	86.14	80.55	74.60	68.36	62.15	56.67	52.01	47.85	44.14	41.05	38.43			
2–3	8.62	12.92	17.86	22.99	28.19	33.18	37.39	40.93	44.06	46.78	48.94	50.69			
4+	0.47	0.94	1.59	2.41	3.45	4.67	5.94	7.06	8.09	9.08	10.01	10.88			
1947															
0–1	91.84	87.28	82.02	76.07	69.78	63.95	58.88	54.25	49.96	46.25	43.02				
2–3	7.75	11.92	16.64	21.85	27.19	31.96	36.05	39.75	43.12	45.93	48.27				
4+	0.41	0.80	1.34	2.08	3.03	4.09	5.07	6.00	6.92	7.82	8.71				
1948															
0–1	92.48	88.22	82.98	77.02	71.14	65.87	60.93	56.22	52.04	48.28					
2–3	7.20	11.14	15.89	21.17	26.22	30.67	34.79	38.67	42.00	44.90					
4+	0.32	0.64	1.13	1.81	2.64	3.46	4.28	5.11	5.96	6.82					
1949															
0–1	92.94	88.75	83.52	77.96	72.77	67.75	62.83	58.33	54.19						
2–3	6.78	10.67	15.43	20.38	24.90	29.22	33.40	37.12	40.45						
4+	0.28	0.58	1.05	1.66	2.33	3.03	3.76	4.55	5.36						
1950															
0–1	93.19	88.98	84.10	79.25	74.34	69.35	64.67	60.25							
2–3	6.57	10.50	14.98	19.33	23.68	28.04	32.03	35.71							
4+	0.24	0.52	0.92	1.42	1.97	2.61	3.30	4.04							
1951															
0–1	93.28	89.33	85.07	80.50	75.64	70.90	66.32								
2–3	6.50	10.21	14.13	18.28	22.64	26.80	30.73								
4+	0.22	0.46	0.80	1.22	1.72	2.30	2.95								

Table B.9. (continued)

Cohorts and Parity Distribution	Age														
	20	21	22	23	24	25	26	27	28	29	30	31	32	33	34
1952															
0–1	93.53	90.05	86.05	81.52	76.89	72.77									
2–3	6.27	9.56	13.28	17.44	21.61	25.68									
4+	0.20	0.39	0.67	1.04	1.50	2.05									
1953															
0–1	93.92	90.64	86.64	82.30	77.80										
2–3	5.91	9.02	12.77	16.76	20.82										
4+	0.17	0.34	0.59	0.94	1.38										
1954															
0–1	94.21	90.90	87.04	82.82											
2–3	5.65	8.81	12.43	16.32											
4+	0.14	0.29	0.53	0.86											
1955															
0–1	94.31	91.09	87.33												
2–3	5.56	8.63	12.16												
4+	0.13	0.28	0.51												

SOURCE: Robert L. Heuser, *Fertility Tables for Birth Cohorts by Color*, DHEW Publication no. (HRA) 76-1152 (Rockville, Md.: National Center for Health Statistics, 1976). Additional data for 1975–1977 provided by NCHS.

[a] Number of children.

Table B.10.   Back-Up Table for Figure 2.11: Cohort Trends in Headship Rates for Population Never Married, 1960–1975

	Year		
Cohort	1960	1970	1975
1956–1960	.000 (0–4)	.0000 (10–14)	.0168 (15–19)[a]
1951–1955	.0000 (5–9)	.0103 (15–19)	.1948 (20–24)
1946–1950	.0000 (10–14)	.1592 (20–24)	.4368 (25–29)
1941–1945	.0064 (15–19)	.3397 (25–29)	.5003 (30–34)
1936–1940	.0885 (20–24)	.3930 (30–34)	.5309 (35–39)
1931–1935	.1953 (25–29)	.4151 (35–39)	.5296 (40–44)
1926–1930	.2661 (30–34)	.4467 (40–44)	.5492 (45–49)
1921–1925	.3194 (35–39)	.4963 (45–49)	.5371 (50–54)
1916–1920	.3656 (40–44)	.5316 (50–54)	.5771 (55–59)
1911–1915	.4293 (45–49)	.5969 (55–59)	.6266 (60–64)
1906–1910	.4834 (50–54)	.6257 (60–64)	.7088 (65–69)
1901–1905	.5100 (55–59)	.6501 (65–69)	.6889 (70–74)
1896–1900	.5606 (60–64)	.6555 (70–74)	.6985 (75–79)
1891–1895	.6015 (65–69)	.6555 (75–79)	.6144 (80–84)
1886–1890	.5913 (70–74)	.6344 (80–84)	****
1881–1885	.5764 (75–79)	****	****
1876–1880	.5695 (80–84)	****	****

SOURCE: Tabulations of 1960 and 1970 Public Use Sample and 1975 Annual Housing Survey Tapes.

[a] Age of cohort in given year in parentheses.

Table B.11. Back-Up Table for Table 2.12: Observed and Projected Headship Rates by Age and Marital Status, 1975–1990

| | Never-Married Men | | | | Never-Married Women | | | |
| | Observed | Projected | | | Observed | Projected | | |
Age	1975	1980	1985	1990	1975	1980	1985	1990
15–19	.0105	.0105	.0105	.0105	.0221	.0297	.0254	.0254
20–24	.2033	.2033	.2033	.2033	.2502	.2691	.2664	.2662
25–29	.4177	.4177	.4177	.4177	.4636	.4971	.4847	.4901
30–34	.4528	.5224	.5224	.5224	.5637	.5562	.5717	.5582
35–39	.5142	.5605	.6164	.6164	.5512	.5928	.5901	.6007
40–44	.5214	.5983	.6367	.6829	.5432	.5666	.6236	.6233
45–49	.5562	.6000	.6644	.6965	.5387	.5791	.6215	.6702
50–54	.5547	.6421	.6776	.7295	.5175	.5943	.6315	.6676
55–59	.5800	.6454	.7151	.7433	.5720	.5914	.6578	.6903
60–64	.6905	.6635	.7161	.7719	.5668	.6465	.6527	.7096
65–69	.7033	.7423	.7200	.7638	.7120	.6405	.6988	.7047
70–74	.7980	.7391	.7737	.7541	.6363	.7482	.6872	.7379
75–79	.7252	.8088	.7539	.7865	.6887	.6837	.7716	.7139
80–84	.7142	.7003	.7818	.7287	.5591	.7081	.6951	.7866
85+	.7647	.6768	.6744	.7530	.5357	.5831	.7253	.7133
Total 15+	.1809	.2121	.2481	.2830	.1993	.2454	.2857	.3162

Table B.11. (continued)

Age	Married Couples[a]				Widowed Women			
	Observed	Projected			Observed	Projected		
	1975	1980	1985	1990	1975	1980	1985	1990
15–19	.8969	.8978	.8981	.8981	—	—	—	.7352
20–24	.9701	.9702	.9699	.9699	.6666	.7349	.7353	.9200
25–29	.9839	.9840	.9838	.9837	.9433	.9241	.9235	.8927
30–34	.9937	.9902	.9907	.9904	.8888	.8949	.8978	.9166
35–39	.9933	.9956	.9940	.9942	.9011	.8727	.9161	.9227
40–44	.9956	.9948	.9964	.9961	.9250	.9194	.8843	.9120
45–49	.9938	.9974	.9974	.9981	.9319	.9383	.9380	.9326
50–54	.9955	.9948	.9982	.9980	.9084	.9307	.9331	.8525
55–59	.9917	.9972	.9965	.9988	.8764	.8298	.8500	.8660
60–64	.9923	.9913	.9972	.9963	.8762	.8898	.8479	.8701
65–69	.9887	.9921	.9911	.9971	.8548	.8941	.9060	.9169
70–74	.9841	.9883	.9918	.9908	.8305	.8717	.9065	.9094
75–79	.9888	.9810	.9856	.9891	.7882	.8353	.8757	.8522
80–84	.9848	.9822	.9758	.9802	.7536	.7673	.8128	.7883
85+	.9558	.9674	.9674	.9661	.5866	.7309	.7440	—
Total 15+	.9874	.9885	.9897	.9908	.8216	.8487	.8636	.8759

Table B.11. (continued)

| Age | All Previously Married Men | | | | Separated/Divorced/Spouse Absent Women | | | |
| | Observed | | Projected | | Observed | | Projected | |
	1975	1980	1985	1990	1975	1980	1985	1990
15–19	.1538	.1538	.1538	.1538	.2419	.1863	.1754	.1754
20–24	.4636	.4636	.4636	.4636	.5684	.5329	.5287	.5285
25–29	.6035	.6035	.6035	.6035	.7592	.7480	.7454	.7398
30–34	.7080	.7124	.7124	.7124	.8632	.8406	.8443	.8382
35–39	.7078	.7915	.7958	.7958	.8857	.8719	.8550	.8557
40–44	.7541	.7916	.8513	.8547	.9076	.8855	.8782	.8637
45–49	.7484	.8225	.8510	.8933	.8723	.9191	.8988	.8932
50–54	.7625	.8321	.8820	.9012	.8398	.8754	.9211	.8999
55–59	.8079	.8444	.8904	.9229	.8524	.8375	.8794	.9229
60–64	.8568	.8685	.8933	.9248	.7673	.8520	.8394	.8810
65–69	.8639	.8891	.8996	.9185	.8392	.7811	.8594	.8470
70–74	.7969	.8895	.9107	.9187	.8388	.8425	.7898	.8647
75–79	.8089	.8290	.9070	.9248	.7964	.8316	.8377	.7872
80–84	.7815	.8130	.8330	.9092	.7656	.7498	.7891	.7952
85+	.6431	.7880	.8188	.8380	.8484	.7006	.6960	.7367
Total 15+	.7401	.7749	.8011	.8247	.8047	.8098	.8175	.8244

SOURCES: Tabulations from 1975 Annual Housing Survey data tape and Joint Center for Urban Studies projections.

[a] According to wife's age.

Appendix C

TABLES RELATING
TO CHAPTER 3

Tables C.1. Back-Up Tables for Figures 3.1 and 3.2

C.1.a. Population by Labor Force Status, 1950 (Percentages)

Age Group	Male			Female		
	Employed	*Unemployed*	*Not in Labor Force*	*Employed*	*Unemployed*	*Not in Labor Force*
0–4	0	0	5.5	0	0	5.3
5–9	0	0	4.5	0	0	4.3
10–14	0	0	3.8	0	0	3.7
15–19	1.3	.2	2.0	.8	.1	2.6
20–24	2.6	.2	.9	1.6	.1	2.2
25–29	3.3	.2	.5	1.3	.1	2.8
30–34	3.3	.1	.3	1.2	.1	2.7
35–39	3.3	.1	.2	1.2	.1	2.5
40–44	3.0	.1	.2	1.2	0	2.2
45–49	2.6	.1	.2	1.0	0	2.0
50–54	2.3	.1	.3	.8	0	1.9
55–59	2.0	.1	.3	.6	0	1.8
60–64	1.5	.1	.4	.4	0	1.6
65–69	.9	.1	.6	.2	0	1.5
70+	.6	.1	1.6	.1	0	2.5
Total	26.7	1.5	21.2	10.4	.5	39.6

SOURCE: U.S. Bureau of the Census, *Census of the Population: 1950*, vol. 2, "Characteristics of the Population," Table 157.

NOTE: Data categories for full-time and part-time employment not available for all years.

Tables C.1. (continued)

C.1.b. Population by Labor Force Status, 1960 (Percentages)

Age Group	Male				Female			
	Employed	Employed Part-Time	Unemployed	Not in Labor Force	Employed	Employed Part-Time	Unemployed	Not in Labor Force
0–4	0	0	0	5.8	0	0	0	5.6
5–9	0	0	0	5.3	0	0	0	5.1
10–14	0	0	0	4.8	0	0	0	4.6
15–19	.5	.8	.2	2.3	.5	.5	.1	2.7
20–24	1.7	.3	.2	.7	1.0	.2	.1	1.7
25–29	2.3	.2	.1	.3	.8	.2	.1	2.0
30–34	2.7	.2	.1	.2	.8	.3	.1	2.2
35–39	2.8	.2	.1	.2	1.0	.4	.1	2.2
40–44	2.6	.2	.1	.2	1.1	.4	.1	1.8
45–49	2.5	.2	.1	.2	1.1	.3	.1	1.6
50–54	2.1	.2	.1	.2	.9	.3	.1	1.5
55–59	1.7	.2	.1	.3	.7	.2	0	1.5
60–64	1.2	.2	.1	.4	.4	.2	0	1.5
65–69	.5	.2	0	.9	.2	.1	0	1.5
70+	.3	.2	0	1.9	.1	.1	0	2.9
Total	20.9	3.1	1.2	23.7	8.6	3.2	.8	38.4

SOURCE: *Census of the Population: 1960. Subject Reports*, "Employment Status and Work Experience," vol. 2:6A, Table 1.

C.1.c. Population by Labor Force Status, 1970 (Percentages)

Age Group	Male				Female			
	Employed	Employed Part-Time	Unemployed	Not in Labor Force	Employed	Employed Part-Time	Unemployed	Not in Labor Force
0–4	0	0	0	4.3	0	0	0	4.1
5–9	0	0	0	5.0	0	0	0	4.8
10–14	0	0	0	5.2	0	0	0	5.0
15–19	.6	1.0	.2	2.1	.5	.7	.2	3.3
20–24	2.0	.5	.2	.7	1.6	.5	.2	1.8
25–29	2.5	.3	.1	.2	1.1	.4	.1	1.8
30–34	2.3	.2	.1	.1	.8	.4	.1	1.6
35–39	2.2	.2	.1	.1	.9	.4	.1	1.5
40–44	2.4	.2	.1	.2	1.1	.4	.1	1.5
45–49	2.4	.2	.1	.2	1.2	.4	.1	1.4
50–54	2.1	.2	.1	.2	1.1	.4	.1	1.4
55–59	1.8	.2	.1	.3	.9	.3	0	1.4
60–64	1.2	.2	0	.5	.6	.2	0	1.4
65–69	.4	.2	0	.9	.2	.1	0	1.6
70+	.5	.2	0	2.2	.1	.1	0	3.6
Total	20.4	3.6	1.1	22.2	10.1	4.3	1.0	36.2

SOURCE: *Census of the Population: 1970*, PC(1)D1, Tables 189 and 215.

Tables C.1. (continued)

C.1.d. Population by Labor Force Status, 1978 (Percentages)

Age Group	Male			Female		
	Employed	Unemployed	Not in Labor Force	Employed	Unemployed	Not in Labor Force
0–4	0	0	3.6	0	0	3.4
5–9	0	0	3.9	0	0	3.8
10–14	0	0	4.3	0	0	4.2
15–19	2.4	.5	1.9	2.0	.4	2.2
20–24	3.4	.3	.6	2.8	.3	1.5
25–29	3.5	.2	.2	2.5	.2	1.5
30–34	3.2	.1	.1	2.0	.1	1.5
35–39	2.6	.1	.1	1.7	.1	1.2
40–44	2.3	.1	.1	1.6	.1	1.0
45–49	2.3	.1	.2	1.5	.1	1.1
50–54	2.2	.1	.3	1.5	.1	1.3
55–59	2.0	.1	.4	1.3	0	1.4
60–64	1.2	0	.8	.7	0	1.5
65–69	.5	0	1.2	.3	0	1.8
70+	.4	0	2.2	.2	0	3.8
Total	26.0	1.6	19.9	18.1	1.4	31.2

SOURCE: U.S. Department of Labor, Bureau of Labor Statistics, "Employment and Unemployment during 1978: An Analysis," Special Labor Force Report no. 218; Current Population Reports, "Population Estimates and Projections," series P-25, no. 800.

Table C.2. **Labor Force Participation Rates of Men and Women Age 16 and Over, 1950–1978**

Year	Men	Women
1950	86.8	33.9
1955	86.2	35.7
1960	84.0	37.8
1965	81.5	39.3
1970	80.6	43.4
1975	78.5	46.4
1978	78.4	51.1

SOURCE: Bureau of Labor Statistics, *Employment and Unemployment during 1978: An Analysis,* no. 218, Table 2.

Tables C.3.   Back-Up Tables for Figure 3.3: Labor Force Participation Rates for Men and Women by Age, 1940–1990

C.3.a.   Single-Year Data in Percentages

| | | | Single-Year Data | | |
| | 1940 | 1950 | 1960 | 1970 | |
Age		Women Only		Women	Men
18	35.4	40.1	43.3	43.8	56.4
19	45.2	47.3	49.9	51.7	64.4
20	47.8	46.9	49.3	55.6	71.4
21	47.7	45.3	47.3	56.2	76.8
22	46.7	43.6	45.8	58.3	82.6
23	44.0	41.0	42.3	57.3	87.2
24	41.4	38.3	39.7	53.2	89.0
25	38.9	32.5	37.5	50.0.	90.7
26	36.7	33.5	35.4	46.7	92.6
27	34.8	32.1	34.4	44.9	93.4
28	34.3	31.2	33.9	43.6	94.1
29	32.5	30.6	33.7	43.0	94.4
30	33.7	31.3	34.2	43.8	94.4
31	30.3	29.8	34.6	43.8	95.3
32	31.3	31.3	35.1	44.4	95.1
33	29.2	30.8	36.0	45.2	95.3
34	29.2	31.6	37.4	45.8	95.3
35	30.2	33.8	38.3	46.7	95.4
36	27.9	32.5	38.6	48.1	95.3
37	27.1	33.2	40.0	48.6	95.3
38	28.2	34.8	41.4	49.6	95.2
39	27.7	34.7	42.4	50.2	95.1
40	28.6	37.7	43.8	51.5	94.8
41	25.0	35.1	44.8	51.9	95.1
42	26.2	36.9	45.3	51.9	94.6
43	24.9	35.9	46.1	53.4	94.6
44	24.2	35.6	46.7	53.3	94.2
45	25.9	37.1	46.8	53.4	94.1
46	23.5	34.5	47.5	53.1	93.8
47	23.0	34.3	47.6	53.3	93.6
48	23.4	34.5	47.4	53.4	93.4
49	22.3	33.4	47.7	53.4	92.9
50	23.7	33.8	47.2	53.3	92.1
51	20.9	30.6	47.0	52.8	91.9
52	20.9	30.6	46.0	52.7	91.9
53	19.8	29.3	44.8	51.8	91.1
54	19.5	28.8	44.2	51.3	90.5
55	19.9	27.9	42.5	49.6	88.9

Table C.3.a. (continued)

Age	Single-Year Data				
	1940	1950	1960	1970	
	Women Only			Women	Men
56	19.2	26.7	40.7	48.7	88.3
57	18.0	25.4	39.7	48.0	86.7
58	17.7	24.8	38.6	46.5	85.8
59	17.4	24.1	37.0	45.1	83.7
60	16.8	23.1	34.7	42.9	81.3
61	15.3	21.0	32.1	40.2	79.2
62	14.9	20.9	29.3	35.9	72.7
63	13.8	19.1	26.1	32.6	67.5
64	12.4	18.0	24.3	29.3	63.1
65	12.0	16.3	20.3	22.0	47.1
66	9.6	13.4	17.6	18.8	41.9
67	8.9	12.2	16.2	17.0	38.6
68	8.2	11.4	14.6	14.7	35.4
69	7.5	10.1	13.2	12.9	31.5
70	6.3	8.1	11.7	9.8	26.9

SOURCES: For 1940, 1950 and 1960: *Census of the Population: 1960,* "Employment Status and Work Experience," Subject Reports, vol. 2:6A. Table 2. For 1970: *Census of the Population: 1970,* PC(1) D1, Tables 189 and 215.

C.3.b.   Percentage of Women in the Labor Force (Grouped Data), 1979 and Projections, 1990

Grouped Data, 1979		Urban Institute Projections, 1990	
Age	Percentages	Age	Percentages
18–19	63.1	16–19	62.1
20–24	69.3	20–24	70.8
25–29	65.8	25–34	71.8
30–34	61.8	35–44	70.2
35–39	63.4	45–54	61.3
40–44	63.9		
45–49	60.4		
50–54	56.5		
55–59	48.7		
60–64	33.9		
65–69	15.3		
70 +	4.7		

SOURCES: Bureau of Labor Statistics, *Employment and Earnings: January 1980,* vol. 27:1, Table 3, "Employment Status of the Non-institutional Population"; Ralph E. Smith, *Women in the Labor Force* (Washington, D.C.: The Urban Institute, 1979).

Table C.4.   **Back-Up Table for Figure 3.4: Labor Force Participation Rates for Birth Cohorts of American Women**

Birth Cohort	Age in Years									
	14–19	20–24	25–29	30–34	35–39	40–44	45–49	50–54	55–59	60–64
1896–1900		37.5[a]		23.6[a]		26.0[a]				
1901–1905	28.4[a]	39.7[f]	30.2[a]	27.2[f]	28.4[a]	31.3[f]	35.0[a]	35.0[a]	39.7[b]	34.7[d]
1906–1910	25.6[f]	41.8[a]	32.9[f]	30.8[a]	31.2[f]	36.6[a]	41.2[a]	45.8[b]	47.3[d]	36.1[c]
1911–1915	22.8[a]	43.7[f]	35.6[a]	31.0[f]	34.0[a]	40.5[a]	47.4[b]	49.4[d]	47.4[c]	34.5[e]
1916–1920	20.9[f]	45.6[a]	34.2[f]	31.2[a]	35.4[a]	45.3[b]	51.2[d]	51.9[c]	47.6[e]	
1921–1925	19.0[a]	44.6[f]	32.8[a]	32.9[a]	40.2[b]	49.6[d]	52.9[c]	53.6[e]		
1926–1930	21.0[a]	43.6[a]	32.4[a]	35.5[b]	43.9[d]	52.1[c]	56.1[e]			
1931–1935	23.0[a]	43.0[a]	35.1[b]	37.9[d]	48.3[c]	57.3[e]				
1936–1940	21.1[a]	44.8[b]	38.6[d]	44.2[c]	55.2[e]					
1941–1945	23.9[b]	49.0[d]	45.4[c]	51.2[e]						
1946–1950	24.8[d]	56.1[c]	56.4[e]							
1951–1955	25.0[c]	62.7[e]								

SOURCE: George S. Masnick, Barbara Wiget, John R. Pitkin, and Dowell Myers, "A Life Course Perspective on the Downturn in U.S. Fertility," *Working Paper* no. 106 (Cambridge, Mass.: Harvard Center for Population Studies, 1978), Table 2.

NOTE: Numbers from sources listed in notes [d] and [e] are not strictly comparable with numbers from those listed in notes [a]–[c] because (1) they are from the CPS rather than the Census; (2) they are from a different enumeration date in April in some cases; (3) they include Alaska and Hawaii; (4) they include members of the Armed Forces stationed overseas; and (5) they do not include inmates of institutions in the population base.

[a] Gertrude Bancroft, *The American Labor Force: Its Growth and Changing Composition* (New York: Wiley, 1958), Table D-1a.

[b] U.S. Bureau of the Census, *U.S. Census of the Population: 1960*, vol. 1:1, "Characteristics of the Population," United States Summary (Washington: GPO, 1964), Table 195.

[c] U.S. Bureau of the Census, *U.S. Census of the Population: 1970*, vol. 1:1, "Characteristics of the Population, United States Summary," Table 215; vol. 1:3, Alaska, Table 164; vol. 1:13, Hawaii, Table 164 (1973).

[d] *Special Labor Force Reports*, no. 69, "Labor Force and Employment in 1965," Tables B-1, B-3.

[e] *Employment and Earnings*, vol. 21 (May 1975), Table A-3.

[f] Derived by straight-line interpolation between the number directly above and the number directly below in the table.

Tables C.5.   Back-Up Tables for Figure 3.5: Labor Force Participation Rates for Selected Birth Cohorts of American Women Age 20–39

1. Single year of age data on women's labor force participation from the 1940, 1950, 1960, and 1970 Censuses were used to derive a single year of age by single year of time matrix through simple linear interpolations (Table C.5.a).
2. Data by five-year age groups (20–24; 25–29; 30–34), and the ten-year age group 35–44 were gathered from the Special Labor Force Reports for the single years 1970 to 1978.
3. Five-year average data were compared with single-year data for ages 22, 27, 32, and 37 for Census years 1940, 1950, 1960, and 1970. Five-year data were judged as reasonable proxies for single-year data at those ages. The five-year data were used to plot points for ages 22, 27, 32, and 39.
4. Projections to 1980 were made from the period data by linear extrapolation based on annual percentage changes from 1960 to 1978. For ages 27, 32, and 39, three estimates were made based on high, medium, and low estimates calculated from the percent change between years. The medium estimate was used in graphing figure 3.5.
5. Linear interpolation between 1970 actual data and 1980 projections were used to estimate single year of age by single year of time rates for 1970 to 1980 (Table C.5.b).
6. Sources for the following are: *U.S. Census of the Population: 1960 Subject Reports*, "Employment Status and Work Experience," Final Report PC(2)-6A (1963); *U.S. Census of the Population: 1970 Subject Reports*, "Employment and Personal Characteristics," Final Report PC9(2)-6A (1973); *Special Labor Force Reports*, "Marital and Family Characteristics of Workers" (1978).

C.5.a. Single Year of Age Labor Force Participation: Linear Interpolation of Census Data

Age	Year									
	1940	1941	1942	1943	1944	1945	1946	1947	1948	1949
20	47.8	47.7	47.6	47.5	47.4	47.3	47.3	47.2	47.1	47.0
21	47.7	47.5	47.2	47.0	46.7	46.5	46.3	46.0	45.8	45.5
22	46.7	46.4	46.0	45.8	45.5	45.2	44.8	44.5	44.2	43.9
23	44.0	43.7	43.4	43.1	42.8	42.5	42.2	41.9	41.6	41.3
24	41.4	41.1	40.8	40.5	40.2	39.9	39.5	39.2	38.9	38.6
25	38.9	38.6	38.2	37.9	37.5	37.2	36.9	36.5	36.2	35.8
26	36.7	36.4	36.1	35.7	35.4	35.1	34.8	34.5	34.1	33.8
27	34.8	34.5	34.3	34.0	33.7	33.5	33.2	32.9	32.6	32.4
28	34.3	34.0	33.7	33.4	33.1	32.8	32.4	32.1	31.8	31.5
29	32.5	32.3	32.1	31.9	31.7	31.6	31.4	31.2	31.0	30.8
30	33.7	33.5	33.2	33.0	32.7	32.5	32.3	32.0	31.8	31.5
31	30.3	30.3	30.2	30.2	30.1	30.1	30.0	30.0	29.9	29.9
32	31.3	31.3	31.3	31.3	31.3	31.3	31.3	31.3	31.3	31.3
33	29.2	29.4	29.5	29.7	29.8	30.0	30.2	30.3	30.5	30.6
34	29.2	29.4	29.7	29.9	30.2	30.4	30.6	30.9	31.1	31.4
35	30.2	30.6	30.9	31.3	31.6	32.0	32.4	32.7	33.1	33.4
36	27.9	28.4	28.8	29.3	29.7	30.2	30.7	31.1	31.6	32.0
37	27.1	27.7	28.3	28.9	29.5	30.2	30.8	31.4	32.0	32.6
38	28.2	28.9	29.5	30.2	30.8	31.5	32.2	32.8	33.5	34.1
39	27.7	28.4	29.1	29.8	30.5	31.2	31.9	32.6	33.3	40.0

C.5.a. (continued)

Age	Year									
	1950	1951	1952	1953	1954	1955	1956	1957	1958	1959
20	46.9	47.1	47.4	47.6	47.9	48.1	48.3	48.6	48.8	49.1
21	45.3	45.5	45.7	45.9	46.1	46.3	46.5	46.7	46.9	47.1
22	43.6	43.8	44.0	44.3	44.5	44.7	44.9	45.1	45.4	45.6
23	41.0	41.1	41.3	41.4	41.5	41.7	41.8	41.9	42.0	42.2
24	38.3	38.4	38.6	38.7	38.9	39.0	39.1	39.3	39.4	39.6
25	35.5	35.7	35.9	36.1	36.3	36.5	36.7	36.9	37.1	37.3
26	33.5	33.7	33.9	34.1	34.3	34.5	34.6	34.8	35.0	35.2
27	32.1	32.3	32.6	32.8	33.0	33.3	33.5	33.7	33.9	34.2
28	31.2	31.5	31.7	32.0	32.3	32.6	32.8	33.1	33.4	33.6
29	30.6	30.9	31.2	31.5	31.8	32.2	32.5	32.8	33.1	33.4
30	31.3	31.6	31.9	32.2	32.5	32.8	33.0	33.3	33.6	33.9
31	29.8	30.3	30.8	31.2	31.8	32.2	32.7	33.2	33.6	34.1
32	31.3	31.7	32.1	32.4	32.8	33.2	33.6	34.0	34.3	34.7
33	30.8	31.3	31.8	32.4	32.9	33.4	33.9	34.4	35.0	35.5
34	31.6	32.2	32.8	33.3	33.9	34.5	35.1	35.7	36.2	36.8
35	33.8	34.3	34.7	35.2	35.6	36.1	36.5	37.0	37.4	37.9
36	32.5	33.1	33.7	34.3	34.9	35.6	36.2	36.8	37.4	38.0
37	33.2	33.9	34.6	35.3	36.0	36.7	37.3	38.0	38.7	39.4
38	34.8	35.5	36.1	36.8	37.4	38.1	38.8	39.4	40.1	40.7
39	34.7	35.5	36.2	37.0	37.8	38.6	39.3	40.1	40.9	41.6

C.5.a. (continued)

Age	Year										
	1960	1961	1962	1963	1964	1965	1966	1967	1968	1969	1970
20	49.3	49.9	50.6	51.2	51.8	52.5	53.1	53.7	54.3	55.0	55.6
21	47.3	48.2	49.1	50.0	50.9	51.8	52.6	53.5	54.4	55.3	56.2
22	45.8	47.1	48.3	49.6	50.8	52.1	53.3	54.6	55.8	57.1	58.3
23	42.3	43.8	45.3	46.8	48.3	49.5	51.3	52.8	54.3	55.8	57.3
24	39.7	41.1	42.4	43.8	45.1	46.5	47.8	49.2	50.5	51.9	53.2
25	37.5	38.8	40.0	41.3	42.5	43.8	45.0	46.3	47.5	48.8	50.0
26	35.4	36.5	37.7	38.8	39.9	41.1	42.2	43.2	44.4	45.6	46.7
27	34.4	35.5	36.5	37.6	38.6	39.7	40.7	41.8	42.8	43.9	44.9
28	33.9	34.9	35.8	36.8	37.8	38.8	39.7	40.7	41.7	42.6	43.6
29	33.7	34.6	35.6	36.5	37.4	38.4	39.3	40.2	41.1	42.1	43.0
30	34.2	35.2	36.1	37.1	38.0	39.0	40.0	40.9	41.9	42.8	43.8
31	34.6	35.5	36.4	37.4	38.3	39.2	40.1	41.0	42.0	42.9	43.8
32	35.1	36.0	37.0	37.9	38.8	39.8	40.7	41.6	42.5	43.5	44.4
33	36.0	36.9	37.8	38.8	39.7	40.6	41.5	42.4	43.4	44.3	45.2
34	37.4	38.2	39.1	39.9	40.8	41.6	42.4	43.3	44.1	45.0	45.8
35	38.3	39.1	40.0	40.8	41.7	42.5	43.3	44.2	45.0	45.9	46.7
36	38.6	39.6	40.5	41.5	42.4	43.4	44.3	45.3	46.2	47.2	48.1
37	40.1	41.0	41.8	42.7	43.5	44.4	45.2	46.1	46.9	47.8	48.6
38	41.4	42.2	43.0	43.9	44.7	45.5	46.3	47.1	48.0	48.8	49.6
39	42.4	43.2	44.0	44.7	45.5	46.3	47.1	47.9	48.6	49.4	50.2

C.5.b.   Interpolated Data 1970 (Actual) to 1980 (Projected)

Age	Year										
	1970	1971	1972	1973	1974	1975	1976	1977	1978	1979	1980
20	55.6	56.6	57.6	58.6	59.6	60.6	61.6	62.6	63.6	64.6	65.6
21	56.2	57.3	58.3	59.4	60.4	61.5	62.6	63.6	64.7	65.7	66.8
22	58.3	59.3	60.2	61.2	62.2	63.2	64.1	65.1	66.1	67.0	68.0
23	57.3	58.3	59.4	60.5	61.6	62.7	63.7	64.8	65.9	66.9	68.6
24	53.2	54.7	56.1	57.6	59.1	60.6	62.0	62.5	65.0	66.4	67.9
25	50.0	51.8	53.6	55.3	57.1	58.9	60.7	62.5	64.2	66.0	67.8
26	46.7	48.8	50.9	53.0	55.1	57.3	59.4	61.5	63.6	65.7	67.8
27	44.9	47.2	49.5	51.7	54.0	56.3	58.6	60.9	63.1	65.4	67.7
28	43.6	46.0	48.3	50.7	53.0	55.4	57.7	60.1	62.4	64.8	67.1
29	43.0	45.4	47.7	50.1	52.4	54.8	57.1	59.5	61.8	64.2	66.5
30	43.8	46.0	48.2	50.5	52.7	54.9	57.1	59.3	61.6	63.8	66.0
31	43.8	46.0	48.1	50.3	52.4	54.6	56.8	58.9	61.1	63.2	65.4
32	44.4	46.4	48.5	50.5	52.6	54.6	56.6	58.7	60.7	62.8	64.8
33	45.2	47.2	49.1	51.1	53.1	55.1	57.0	59.0	61.0	62.9	64.9
34	45.8	47.7	49.7	51.6	53.5	55.5	57.4	59.3	61.2	63.2	65.1
35	46.7	48.6	50.4	52.3	54.1	56.0	57.8	59.7	61.5	63.4	65.2
36	48.1	49.8	51.6	53.3	55.0	56.8	58.5	60.2	61.9	63.7	65.4
37	48.6	50.3	52.0	53.7	55.4	57.1	58.7	60.4	62.1	63.8	65.5
38	49.6	51.2	52.8	54.4	56.0	57.7	59.3	60.9	62.5	64.1	65.7
39	50.2	51.8	53.3	54.9	56.4	58.0	59.6	61.1	62.7	64.2	65.8

Tables C.6.   Back-Up Tables for Figure 3.6: Labor Force Participation Rates for Selected Groups of Women, 1950–1978

C.6.a.   Women's Labor Force Participation Rates by Marital Status

	Census Years			
Age	1940	1950	1960	1970
20–24	45.6	42.9	44.9	56.1
Single	73.1	73.3	73.2	69.6
Married	17.3	26.0	31.1	46.6
Other Marital Status	57.0	54.3	53.9	61.0
25–29	35.5	32.6	35.0	45.4
Single	79.5	79.8	79.1	79.3
Married	18.5	22.1	26.8	38.0
Other Marital Status	63.9	59.3	58.2	63.1
30–34	30.9	31.0	35.5	44.2
Single	77.7	77.9	79.4	76.4
Married	17.6	22.5	29.0	38.8
Other Marital Status	66.6	62.4	62.2	63.9

SOURCES: *Current Population Reports*, "Marital Status and Family Status: April 1955," series P-20, No. 62 (December 1955); *Special Labor Force Reports*, "Marital and Family Characteristics of Workers: March 1960," no. 13 (April 1961); "Marital and Family Characteristics of Workers: March 1970," no. 130 (March 1971); *U.S. Census of the Population: 1930*, "Occupations by States," vol. 4 (1933); *U.S. Census of the Population: 1950*, "Employment and Personal Characteristics," vol. 4:1a, Special Reports (1953); *U.S. Census of the Population: 1960 Subject Reports*, "Employment Status and Work Experience," Final Report PC(2)-6A (1963); *U.S. Census of the Population: 1970 Subject Reports*, "Employment and Personal Characteristics," Final Report PC(2)-6A (1973).

C.6.b. Participation Rates of Women with Children, Husband Present, 1965–1977

	Year			
Age	1965[a]	1970	1975	1977
16–24				
With Children under Age 18	22.6	32.5	38.1	41.4
With Children under Age 6	22.4	32.1	38.0	41.1
25–34				
With Children under Age 18	28.2	35.3	42.6	45.9
With Children under Age 6	24.1	29.6	36.8	39.2
35–44				
With Children under Age 8	36.7	44.8	50.3	54.4
With Children under Age 6	22.7	30.4	34.0	37.0
45+				
With Children under Age 18	38.6	44.7	44.9	47.0
With Children under Age 6	22.9	28.2	30.6	31.8

SOURCES: U.S. Department of Labor, Bureau of Labor Statistics, *Special Labor Force Reports*, "Marital and Family Characteristics of Workers, March 1965," no. 64 (March 1966); "Marital and Family Characteristics of Workers, March 1970," no. 130 (March 1971); "Marital and Family Characteristics, March 1975, no. 183 (November 1975); "Marital and Family Characteristics of Workers, March 1977," no. 216.

[a] The category, 16–24, includes 14- and 15-year-olds for 1965 only.

Table C.7. Back-Up Table for Figure 3.7: Labor Force Participation in 1978 and Work Experience in 1977

Sex	Age							
	18–19	20–24	25–34	35–44	45–54	55–59	60–64	65+
Men								
LFP, 1978	67.6	83.9	95.1	95.6	91.3	82.9	60.9	19.6
Worked in 1977	83.6	91.1	95.8	95.9	92.2	85.9	70.1	26.7
YRFT in 1977	13.4	38.9	70.9	78.3	75.8	68.3	47.7	8.3
YRFT ÷ WX	16.0	42.7	74.0	81.6	82.2	79.5	68.0	30.9
LFP ÷ WX	78.1	92.1	99.3	99.7	99.0	96.5	86.9	73.4
Women								
LFP, 1978	57.8	66.0	61.9	61.8	56.7	48.7	33.6	8.4
Worked in 1977	73.5	76.7	68.1	66.1	61.7	54.2	40.6	12.0
YRFT in 1977	9.4	27.7	32.1	32.4	32.8	31.1	18.8	2.4
YRFT ÷ WX	12.8	36.1	47.2	48.9	53.2	57.3	46.3	19.6
LFP ÷ WX	78.6	86.0	90.9	93.5	91.9	89.9	82.8	70.0

SOURCE: *Special Labor Force Reports*. "Work Experience of the Population in 1977," no. 224.

NOTE: LFP —Labor force participation
YRFT—Year round, full time
WX —Work experience

Table C.8. **Back-Up Table for Figure 3.8: Percentage of Women Working Year-Round Full-Time by Age, 1960–1977**

	Age					
Year	*18–19*	*20–24*	*25–34*	*35–44*	*45–54*	*55–59*
1960	12.1	22.4	16.5	22.9	27.1	24.0
1965	9.4	25.6	19.2	25.0	28.3	27.8
1970	8.2	25.6	22.7	26.9	32.9	31.6
1975	9.6	26.0	29.1	29.0	31.3	29.2
1977	9.4	27.7	32.1	32.3	32.8	31.1

SOURCES: U.S. Department of Labor, Bureau of Labor Statistics, *Special Labor Force Reports*, "Marital and Family Characteristics of Workers, March 1960," no. 13 (April 1961); "Marital and Family Characteristics of Workers, March 1965," no. 64 (March 1966); "Marital and Family Characteristics of Workers, March 1970," no. 130 (March 1971); "Marital and Family Characteristics, March 1975," no. 183 (November 1975); "Marital and Family Characteristics of Workers, 1970–1978," no. 219 (April 1979).

Table C.9. Back-Up Table for Figure 3.9: Work Experience of Married Women, Husband Present, with Children, 1960–1978

	Percentages of Married Women					
	Full-Time Workers			*Part-Time Workers*		
Number of Children	*50–52 weeks*	*27–49 weeks*	*0–26 weeks*	*27–52 weeks*	*0–26 weeks*	*Total with Work Experience*
Children Age 6–17 Only						
1960	16.0	8.5	7.6	11.2	6.7	50.0
1965	18.7	8.2	6.4	11.7	8.0	53.1
1970	23.3	7.2	6.8	12.5	7.6	57.5
1975	24.4	7.3	5.6	15.1	6.8	59.3
1978	26.3	6.7	6.1	16.4	8.0	63.5
Children Age 3–5, None under Age 3						
1960	9.6	5.6	8.1	7.4	7.1	37.8
1965	10.0	6.3	8.3	7.9	8.1	40.7
1970	14.2	6.3	8.4	10.4	8.3	47.7
1975	17.6	6.8	7.8	10.4	8.5	51.0
1978	17.9	7.5	7.9	10.4	10.6	54.3
Children under Age 3						
1960	3.4	5.6	10.4	4.0	7.7	31.1
1965	4.2	7.2	11.4	4.8	7.8	35.4
1970	6.5	7.4	13.9	5.7	8.4	41.9
1975	10.0	8.3	11.2	6.0	11.0	46.5
1978	10.0	9.4	12.5	7.9	10.3	50.1

SOURCES: Same as those for Table C.6.b.

Table C.10. **Back-Up Table for Figure 3.10: Types of Households and Employment with Mean Income, 1977**

Male Primary Individuals not Full-Time (n = 421,013)

Age	Income
Total	$6,690
18–24	5,907
25–34	7,867
35–44	9,313
45–54	6,096
55–64	7,747
65 +	5,665

Female Primary Individuals not Full-Time (n = 819,800)

Age	Income
Total	$5,080
18–24	4,249
25–34	7,110
35–44	7,651
45–54	5,257
55–64	4,994
65 +	4,968

Male Primary Individuals Full-Time (n = 360,087)

Age	Income
Total	$15,206
18–24	10,618
25–34	14,622
35–44	17,945
45–54	17,363
55–64	15,859
65 +	15,184

Female Primary Individuals Full-Time (n = 306,300)

Age	Income
Total	$10,855
18–24	7,957
25–34	11,290
35–44	12,606
45–54	12,027
55–64	10,932
65 +	10,846

Male Family Head not Full-Time (n = 72,686)

Age	Income
Total	$12,789
18–24	Base too low
25–34	11,691
35–44	11,412
45–54	18,786
55–64	14,330
65 +	Base too low

Female Family Head not Full-Time (n = 550,989)

Age	Income
Total	$7,840
18–24	3,833
25–34	5,058
35–44	7,251
45–54	9,506
55–64	9,950
65 +	Base too low

Table C.10. (continued)

Male Family Head Full-Time (n = 86,713)		Female Family Head Full-Time (n = 272,611)	
Age	Income	Age	Income
Total	$19,345	Total	$13,795
18–24	Base too low	18–24	10,366
25–34	17,678	25–34	10,960
35–44	19,169	35–44	14,019
45–54	21,298	45–54	16,430
55–64	20,500	55–64	15,769
65+	Base too low	65+	Base too low

Husband-Wife

Husband Full-Time, Wife Employed (n = 1,532,076)		Husband Full-Time, Wife not Employed (n = 1,491,311)	
Age	Income	Age	Income
Total	$24,726	Total	$21,982
18–24	16,340	18–24	12,345
25–34	21,646	25–34	18,148
35–44	25,625	35–44	22,885
45–54	28,338	45–54	25,547
55–64	26,523	55–64	23,734
65+	26,783	65+	23,690

Husband not Full-Time, Wife Employed (n = 546,742)		Husband not Full-Time, Wife not Employed (n = 1,053,589)	
Age	Income	Age	Income
Total	$16,255	Total	$11,803
18–24	11,279	18–24	7,618
25–34	14,849	25–34	11,186
35–44	18,654	35–44	13,951
45–54	18,620	45–54	15,013
55–64	18,941	55–64	13,452
65+	14,371	65+	10,880

SOURCE: *Current Population Reports,* "Consumer Income," series P-60, no. 118 (March 1979), Tables 20 and 21.

NOTE: Numbers in parentheses are the Current Population Survey total for the category.

Table C.11. Back-Up Table for Table 3.4: Proportion of Married Women Age 18–47 (born 1921–1950) Earning Greater than 20 and 33 Percent of Family Income for Specific Lengths of Time, 1968–1977

Years with Earnings >20%	Years in Labor Force										
	0	1	2	3	4	5	6	7	8	9	10
0	100.0	90.5	69.0	54.7	44.9	48.6	23.2	18.3	17.0	13.6	6.4
1	0	9.5	21.4	18.6	24.4	12.2	17.4	8.5	10.0	5.9	1.9
2	0	0	9.5	19.8	14.1	10.8	18.8	12.2	7.0	11.0	0.8
3	0	0	0	7.0	12.8	12.2	11.6	11.0	6.0	5.1	4.2
4	0	0	0	0	3.8	9.5	18.8	12.2	7.0	7.6	2.7
5	0	0	0	0	0	6.8	5.8	13.4	12.0	5.1	3.0
6	0	0	0	0	0	0	4.3	13.4	16.0	11.0	7.6
7	0	0	0	0	0	0	0	11.0	13.0	13.6	7.2
8	0	0	0	0	0	0	0	0	12.0	16.9	14.4
9	0	0	0	0	0	0	0	0	0	10.2	17.8
10	0	0	0	0	0	0	0	0	0	0	34.1
$n =$	228	105	84	86	78	74	69	82	100	118	264

Table C.11. (continued)

Years with Earnings >33%	Years in Labor Force										
	0	1	2	3	4	5	6	7	8	9	10
0	100.0	95.2	84.5	81.4	71.8	68.9	56.5	46.3	46.0	38.1	22.7
1	0	4.8	13.1	8.1	19.2	10.8	23.2	17.1	9.0	11.9	11.7
2	0	0	2.4	9.3	3.8	9.5	8.7	9.8	8.0	10.2	6.1
3	0	0	0	1.2	5.1	5.4	7.2	12.2	9.0	6.8	8.3
4	0	0	0	0	0	5.4	4.3	4.9	8.0	6.8	7.2
5	0	0	0	0	0	0	0	1.2	6.0	6.8	6.8
6	0	0	0	0	0	0	0	3.7	5.0	3.4	7.2
7	0	0	0	0	0	0	0	4.9	7.0	6.8	6.8
8	0	0	0	0	0	0	0	0	2.0	5.9	6.4
9	0	0	0	0	0	0	0	0	0	3.4	6.4
10	0	0	0	0	0	0	0	0	0	0	10.2
$n =$	228	105	84	86	78	74	69	82	100	118	264

SOURCE: Tabulations from the Panel Study of Income Dynamics by Neal Baer.

Table C.12.   Back-Up Table for Figures 3.11 and 3.12: Mean Income of Women with Children by Income Thirds during Marriage (1967 Dollars)

	Income Third				
Years of Work	*Total*	*1*	*2*	*3*	*n*
	Women Ever Divorced				
Married	10,678	5,535	10,188	16,251	199
Break	7,267	5,615	6,681	9,487	199
Year after Break					
1	6,064	4,569	5,367	8,005	176
2	6,477	4,744	6,237	8,122	134
3	6,654	4,845	5,708	9,011	99
	Women Separated, Never Divorced				
Married		4,095	6,938	13,200	135
Break		3,810	5,606	9,823	135
Year after Break					
1		2,581	3,153	6,208	73
2		2,257	3,536	4,816	29
3		3,020	3,751	5,999	19
	Widowed Women				
Married		3,669	7,713	15,172	49
Break		3,807	6,927	12,283	49
Year after Break					
1		4,841	4,916	8,541	47
2		4,833	4,217	8,290	39
3		5,408	4,538	8,119	32

SOURCE: Tabulations from the Panel Study of Income Dynamics by Nancy Goodban.

Table C.13. Back-Up Table for Table 3.6: Proportion of Unmarried Women Age 18–47 (born 1921–1950) Earning Greater than 20, 33, 50, and 75 Percent of Family Income for Specific Lengths of Time, 1968–1977

Years with Earnings >20%	Years in Labor Force										
	0	1	2	3	4	5	6	7	8	9	10
0	100.0	68.8	42.1	22.2	23.1	27.3	20.0	14.3	0	0	0
1	0	31.3	15.8	16.7	7.7	0	10.0	0	4.3	0	0
2	0	0	42.1	27.8	7.7	9.1	0	0	0	3.8	0.6
3	0	0	0	33.3	15.4	18.2	20.0	0	8.7	0	0
4	0	0	0	0	46.2	9.1	20.0	0	8.7	3.8	0
5	0	0	0	0	0	36.4	10.0	0	8.7	3.8	0
6	0	0	0	0	0	0	20.0	71.4	4.3	7.7	1.3
7	0	0	0	0	0	0	0	14.3	17.4	3.8	3.2
8	0	0	0	0	0	0	0	0	47.8	19.2	1.9
9	0	0	0	0	0	0	0	0	0	57.7	13.0
10	0	0	0	0	0	0	0	0	0	0	79.9

Years with Earnings >33%											
	0	1	2	3	4	5	6	7	8	9	10
0	100.0	75.0	42.1	33.3	38.5	36.4	40.0	14.3	4.3	0	0.6
1	0	25.0	47.4	11.1	7.7	0	0	0	8.7	7.7	0.6
2	0	0	10.5	27.8	30.8	18.2	0	0	8.7	3.8	0
3	0	0	0	27.8	7.7	9.1	20.0	14.3	4.3	3.8	0
4	0	0	0	0	15.4	18.2	10.0	28.6	13.0	3.8	1.9
5	0	0	0	0	0	18.2	10.0	0	4.3	7.7	3.9
6	0	0	0	0	0	0	20.0	42.9	13.0	0	3.9
7	0	0	0	0	0	0	0	0	8.7	3.8	3.9
8	0	0	0	0	0	0	0	0	34.8	23.1	4.5
9	0	0	0	0	0	0	0	0	0	46.2	15.6
10	0	0	0	0	0	0	0	0	0	0	64.9
n =	44	16	19	18	13	11	10	7	23	26	154

Table C.13. (continued)

Years with Earnings >50%					Years in Labor Force						
	0	1	2	3	4	5	6	7	8	9	10
0	100.0	87.5	63.2	50.0	46.2	36.4	40.0	14.3	13.0	3.8	0.6
1	0	12.5	31.6	33.3	15.4	18.2	10.0	0	13.0	7.7	5.8
2	0	0	5.3	0	23.1	0	0	28.6	8.7	11.5	1.9
3	0	0	0	16.7	15.4	18.2	10.0	0	0	0	5.2
4	0	0	0	0	0	9.1	20.0	14.3	13.0	3.8	5.2
5	0	0	0	0	0	18.2	10.0	42.9	8.7	3.8	2.6
6	0	0	0	0	0	0	10.0	0	13.0	7.7	3.9
7	0	0	0	0	0	0	0	0	4.3	11.5	4.5
8	0	0	0	0	0	0	0	0	26.1	26.9	4.5
9	0	0	0	0	0	0	0	0	0	23.1	17.5
10	0	0	0	0	0	0	0	0	0	0	48.1

Years with Earnings >75%											
	0	1	2	3	4	5	6	7	8	9	10
0	100.0	93.8	73.7	77.8	76.9	63.6	50.0	42.9	26.1	23.1	10.4
1	0	6.3	26.3	5.6	23.1	9.1	10.0	14.3	21.7	7.7	6.5
2	0	0	0	16.7	0	0	10.0	14.3	4.3	7.7	9.1
3	0	0	0	0	0	9.1	10.0	14.3	13.0	7.7	3.2
4	0	0	0	0	0	9.1	0	14.3	4.3	0	3.2
5	0	0	0	0	0	9.1	20.0	0	8.7	11.5	5.2
6	0	0	0	0	0	0	0	0	4.3	19.2	5.2
7	0	0	0	0	0	0	0	0	8.7	11.5	8.4
8	0	0	0	0	0	0	0	0	8.7	7.7	10.4
9	0	0	0	0	0	0	0	0	0	3.8	12.3
10	0	0	0	0	0	0	0	0	0	0	26.0
n =	44	16	19	18	13	11	10	7	23	26	154

SOURCE: Tabulations of Panel Study of Income Dynamics, 1968–1977, by Neal Baer.

Table C.14. Back-Up Table for Figure 3.13: Ratio of Earnings of Employed
Women to Earnings of Employed Men, 1970 and 1977

| | Year-Round, Full-Time Workers | | |
Ages	Men	Women	Ratio
1970			
18–24	5467	4340	79.4
25–34	8601	5069	58.9
35–44	9640	4832	50.1
45–54	9310	4881	52.4
55–64	8225	4698	57.1
All	7350	4786	65.1
1977			
18–24	9497	7338	77.3
25–29	13,287	9500	71.5
30–34	16,220	9625	59.3
35–39	18,322	9830	53.7
40–44	18,568	9333	50.3
45–49	18,720	9653	51.6
50–54	18,308	9541	52.1
55–59	17,365	9338	53.8
60–64	16,309	9054	55.5
65+	14,649	7604	51.9
All	16,171	9133	56.5

SOURCES: For 1970: *U.S. Census of the Population: 1970*, "Occupation and Industry," series PC(2)-7A, Table 23. For 1977: *Current Population Reports*, "Money Income in 1977 of Families and Persons in the United States, 1979," series P-60, no. 118 (March 1979), Table 48.

Table C.15. Back-Up Table for Figure 3.14: Transfer Payments and Benefits as a Percentage of Total Personal Income, 1950–1976

Income Source	Year						
	1950	1955	1960	1965	1970	1975	1976
Personal Income ($1,000s)	226,102	308,796	399,724	537,031	801,271	1,253,367	1,382,698
Benefits							
OASDHI and Railroad Retirement	1,226,478	5,416,099	12,022,954	19,226,930	33,325,978	69,868,371	78,902,533
Retirement	828,334	4,083,622	8,790,577	13,246,830	22,188,057	44,610,962	50,216,042
Disability	77,315	103,089	714,915	1,722,668	3,286,338	8,816,923	10,386,544
Survivors	320,829	1,229,388	2,517,462	4,257,432	7,851,583	16,440,486	18,299,947
Percentage	0.5	1.8	3.0	3.6	4.2	5.6	5.7
Veterans Retirement, Disability, & Survivors	2,223,787	2,745,941	3,436,883	4,195,962	5,480,096	7,668,188	8,409,231
Percentage	1.0	0.9	0.9	0.8	0.7	0.6	0.6
Workmen's Compensation	532,360	835,618	1,228,198	1,680,703	2,701,787	5,464,977	6,134,025
Percentage	0.2	0.3	0.3	0.3	0.3	0.4	0.4
Unemployment	1,467,570	1,560,175	3,024,741	2,451,558	4,353,343	18,030,191	16,304,569
Percentage	0.6	0.5	0.8	0.5	0.5	1.4	1.2
Lump-Sum Benefits	86,693	195,622	299,503	420,540	582,173	807,830	863,707
Percentage	[a]	0.1	0.1	0.1	0.1	0.1	0.1
Total Benefits	5,536,888	10,743,455	20,012,279	27,975,693	46,443,377	101,839,557	110,614,047
Percentage	2.4	3.5	5.0	5.2	5.8	8.1	8.0

Table C.15. (continued)

Income Source	1950	1955	1960	1965	1970	1975	1976
Transfers							
SSI Assistance							
Aged	1,461,624	1,490,352	1,629,541	1,600,708	1,862,412	b	b
Blind	52,698	67,958	86,231	85,121	98,292	b	b
Disabled	7,967	135,168	237,366	417,720	999,861	b	b
Total	1,522,289	1,693,478	1,953,138	2,103,549	2,960,565	5,716,072	5,900,215
Percentage	0.7	0.5	0.5	0.4	0.4	0.5	0.4
AFDC	551,653	617,841	1,000,784	1,660,186	4,852,464	9,211,355	9,999,870
General Assistance	298,262	214,266	322,465	259,225	618,319	1,138,211	1,227,866
Food Stamps	—	—	—	32,494	550,806	4,386,144	5,310,133
Public Assistance							
Total	849,915	832,107	1,323,249	1,951,905	6,022,089	14,735,710	16,537,869
Percentage	0.4	0.3	0.3	0.4	0.8	1.2	1.2
SSI + Public							
Assistance Percentage	1.1	0.8	0.8	0.8	1.2	1.7	1.6
Total Benefits Percentage	2.4	3.5	5.0	5.2	5.8	8.1	8.0
TOTAL PERCENTAGE	3.5	4.3	5.8	6.0	7.0	9.8	9.6

Year (column group header over 1950–1976)

SOURCE: Social Security Administration, *Social Security Bulletin*, Annual Statistical Supplement (1976), Tables 16, 169, 147, 168, 170, and 29.
[a] Less than 0.1 percent.
[b] Not available.

Table C.16. Poverty Rates for Persons below the Poverty Level, 1959–1977

	Year				
	1959	*1964*	*1969*	*1974*	*1977*
All Persons	22.4	19.0	12.1	11.6	11.6
Persons over 65	35.2	—	25.3	15.7	14.1
Persons in Female-Headed Families	50.2	45.9	38.4	34.4	32.8
Male Unrelated Individuals over 65	59.0	—	39.8	26.8	23.6
Female Unrelated Individuals over 65	63.3	—	49.9	31.9	28.4
Wives over 65	30.5	—	17.2	8.3	7.5

SOURCE: *Current Population Survey,* "Characteristics of the Population below the Poverty Level: 1977," series P-60, no. 119, (March 1979), Tables 1 and 3.